STALKED BY A PI

Stalked by a PI

"Cyberbullying & Defamation"

JOLENE K. JOHNSON

True Life Publishing All Rights Reserved Copyright © May 2020

CONTENTS

COPYRIGHT
vii
DEDICATION
viii

~ one ~
Brief Encounter
1

~ two ~
"Employment Transition"
5

~ three ~
"Online - Real Life Collide"
16

~ four ~
"The Police Investigation"
26

~ five ~
Commencing Litigation
31

~ six ~
Who is Lee Hanlon?
37

~ seven ~
The Trial
41

~ eight ~
The Regulatory Complaints
55

~ nine ~
Emotional Toll
62

~ ten ~
The Aftermath
67

~ eleven ~
Court Judgement
70

~ twelve ~
Epilague
222

Copyright © 2020 by Jolene K. Johnson True Life Publishing

All rights reserved. No part of this book may be reproduced in any manner whatsoever without written permission except in the case of brief quotations embodied in critical articles and reviews.

First Printing, 2020

This book is dedicated to all the men and women, and businesses alike, that have been survivors of online bullying and personal attacks.

I wrote this book, not for sympathy, but to provide courage to those who have been through similar circumstances as I. Words are powerful, but you are powerful too!.

I wish to thank my friends, family and business associates that have been there for me through the good and the bad. I could never have made it without your love and support, and your belief in me.

~ One ~

BRIEF ENCOUNTER

I have always thought of myself as someone who believes in people, believes in justice. I guess this is why the story of a single father who had a nine year old daughter with autism, taken away by social services, our local child protection agency caught my eye.

The story was all over the news, and of course the social media site Facebook.com. There were fundraising campaigns set up to help pay for legal expenses to assist the father with any court cases that occurred as a result of the social workers removal. There were many not for profit support groups and advocates chomping at the bit to help the family seek justice.

For many days I would read various articles, and comments of support for the family, and this is how I came to be in a Facebook.com chat group. In this group people would make a series of posts about the families situation and you can also message individual users. As this book is not about that story, I have not posted the names of the family in respect for their privacy. Their case hit international headlines. It was at this time that I started receiving a Facebook message from a stranger.

The Facebook.com group became a forum for parents all over the world to connect and discuss their own injustices at the hands of the child protection agencies. Stories, emerged with parents telling their tale of how their children had been wrongfully removed and they were good parents. I guess this is how I got caught up in all of this. As I too had a story to share, a story of my own injustice at the hands of rouge social workers.

Initially, when I joined the group it was more out of pure interest as the case itself was unique given the families circumstances. I was mostly just reading comments and not really posting much. It was in this forum I shared a part of my own story, of when my children were wrongfully apprehended a year prior. At the time I was litigating against the government for wrongfully removing my children. It was at this time I received a message from a stranger, claiming to be an advocate and wanting to help me with my case.

I received a message from a user profile named "Lee Hanlon", the user went on to state how he was wanting to offer me legal advice and help with my court case against the Ministry for Children & Families. The user went on to tell me how he was a first year law student, and how he was an advocate for families torn apart by the system. He would continue on to tell me how he was a 17 year veteran of the Canadian Military, and he was trying to become a private investigator. He would tell me that he could represent me in court and help prepare all my documents for my upcoming court matter. I really didn't know this guy, and I was a bit concerned that he had messaged me randomly of all people which I thought was odd. To me he was just a Facebook user, and we had some common interests which was the case that the group was all about.

It is quite typical to have private messages from user profiles unknown to you on Facebook. It is a way to connect with people even people you do not know that sometimes share the same interests that you do.

The messages were far few and between approximately nine or ten messages back and forth, at this time I was really not sure of who the user really was that was messaging me as he was not a lawyer, and he seemed to know information that I had not shared publicly, I declined to speak with him, and asked him if he was working for MCFD. The user then got very irate with their messages. I then blocked the user using the blocking feature, as I wished no contact further as this user seemed very odd. Thinking that this would be the end of contact with this profile named "Lee Hanlon", I did not think about him any longer. After all he was just some random profile that messaged me on facebook, as I received messages all the time from people I did not know. Little did I know I would meet him online once again 5 years later.

At this time I truly did not realize how much of an impact "Lee Hanlon" would have on my life both personal and professional. I had no idea that by responding to his message through facebook, although it was an innocent communication, just two people talking about the same topic of interest, would be the foundation for someones twisted and disturbing fascination and obsession towards me. Had I known this, I most certainly would have taken precautions online. Hindsight is 2020 they say. You never know the true dangerous of the online world, until something happens.

~ Two ~

"EMPLOYMENT TRANSITION"

Ever since I was a child, I always wanted to become a private investigator. I was curious about everything around me. I was always up in other people's business. I was always told to mind my business, however, I was not very good at it. I thought I could save the world. I was always the type of girl, who wanted to know why things happened, how it happened and how you can fix a problem if there was one. Everyone had a story to tell, and I was interested in hearing them.

You see I grew up in the seventies, I entered this world with many medical complications. I was born without an esophagus. This led to me being hospitalized for the first 2 1/2 years of my life. Born, in Vancouver, British Columbia, Canada, I was fortunate to have the most excellent medical care. Unfortunately though, I ended up being placed in foster care at the age of three, as the government didn't think my parents were equipped to raise me with the onslaught of medical conditions I had been born with.

When I was six, I finally was able to meet my biological parents Karen & Bill, for the first time and then there was my sister who was two years older. We lived in a large three story house on Main Street, right beside the business Produce City. After living there for a few years, my family eventually decided to relocate to Prince George, British Columbia, where my father worked as a truck driver, for a furniture moving company, and my mother was a stay at home mom raising my sister and I. This happy family unit did not last very long, as before I knew it, I was subjected to physical abuse by my mother, which led me to being apprehended by social workers at the age of eight. The weird thing is my sister was never taken.

As I spent my entire childhood in foster care, jumping from foster home to foster home in my early years, and then once I turned twelve, I entered group homes, and was transferred throughout many different group homes. I was housed with many other children older than I, which subjected me to both physical and sexual abuse.

While I was living in the homes, the social workers failed to do anything about the abuse, leaving me in the homes with my abusers. I guess this is when I started realizing there were so many injustices in the world. I always wanted to help people. Other kids in the homes I was in would start fighting and I was always nosy trying to figure out what caused the fight and would try to fix the problems.

I was an avid reader as well, and my favourite book was Harriet the Spy. I always wanted to be like her. I would carry a notebook around with me writing down what I saw. People would get annoyed with me. So I guess I was always meant to be a private investigator.

One would think that being a private investigator would have been my first occupation. Nope, I decided to work in the restaurant industry, went through probably every fast food chain there is and I hated it. I then moved on to working as a loss prevention officer. My job was to observe and apprehend shoplifters, I absolutely loved it. I then had a job at a collection agency and started skip-tracing. This was in the early nineties, and it turned out I had a knack for skip tracing. I was so good at finding people, and it was fun tracking people, via telephone and back then it was much different as to the way skip-tracing is done. This was before the privacy act was established, now skip-tracing, although I am good at it the tools for the trade are vastly different than in the nineties. It was at this time I opened my first business, North American Tracing. I operated in a little hole in the wall office down on Hornby Street, in downtown Vancouver.

It was at this time as well I met my later to be husband Derek. Derek, and I, met and then decided to get married within three weeks of knowing each other. We had a very small intimate wedding in the Esther's Inn Hotel, in Prince George, British Columbia. Unfortunately my father did not attend, which I really struggled with. Married life, was very short-lived as shortly after my wedding to Derek, who was twenty years my senior, he was diagnosed with stage four terminal brain cancer, and within three weeks of his diagnosis, my father, also was diagnosed with terminal brain and lung cancer. They both succumbed to their illnesses in February and March of 1997.

Just as I thought my life was on track, it felt like I was hit with a freight train, and I emotionally took a beating landing me in a deep dark hole emotionally. I was still dealing with the emotional nightmare of being sexually abused during my childhood, and now with this on top of it, I had an emotional breakdown. I eventually pulled out of it, about three years later.

It was at this time I started to get my life back on track. During the three years of emotional hell, I had dabbled in cocaine and ended up overdosing, and almost lost my life due to my poor decision making. Realizing that this truly was not the life I wanted to lead, as I knew that I wanted to be a successful member of society, I knew I had to do something to change my life around, if I didn't want to become a statistic as most children who grow up in foster care did. I decided to enrol in a correspondence course, which indirectly led me to meeting the future father of my children.

In the year 2000, I met a very handsome First Nations man, he was visiting a neighbour who resided in my apartment building. We were inseparable. I fell in love with him. To this day, I do not think he truly knew how I felt about him. We decided to have a child, and I managed to get pregnant with our first daughter, who was born in the spring of 2001. Unfortunately, he decided to move back to Winnipeg, Manitoba, and left me to raise our daughter as a single mother. His absence was short-lived as our daughter had some minor medical problems, and he returned when she was briefly stolen from me by my mother who I had decided to move in with to give me a hand. The toxic relationship between my mother and I, really hadn't changed as I had hoped it would have. I was at work one night, and when I returned to our shared duplex, I found out my mother went behind my back and obtained sole custody of my daughter who was nine months old at the time.

For a period of about two weeks I had to fight with my mom to get custody of my daughter again. This led to social workers apprehending from my mother, and my daughter's father returned to join the fight. It was during his return that we got pregnant with our second daughter. Our second daughter was not exactly planned, and she ended up being born three months premature and had to spend the first three months of her life hospitalized. My girl's father and I tried to make it work between us, and coparent our children together, however it did not work out and we separated in 2004.

Once again, I was a single mom but this time with two girls. I then opened up my second skip-tracing agency, as my previous company North American Tracing in Vancouver, shut down and I had to file bankruptcy years before. Now I opened People Locators Canada., I had a large three thousand square foot office, in the downtown core of Prince George. I truly thought that I had found my calling, as I was able to hire approximately one hundred staff members, we had vending machines for the employees, and my mother worked for me as we had ironed out our differences or so I thought.

This company to ended up flopping, as I had left my children's father, and my business partner turned into a psychotic stalker, so I ended up relocating to Aldergrove, BC, with the girls. Shortly, after in 2007, my mother also relocated to Langley, British Columbia, and we were able to recommence a mother daughter relationship as adults.

After I relocated to Aldergrove, I opened up another skip-tracing company National People Locator. I had a couple of staff but nothing massive. I then decided to open a used children's clothing store called Kidsville, the issue with this is two days before I opened the City of Langley refused to give me a business license. I was never really informed as to why, so to this day I have no clue why they refused. I hated living in Aldergrove and eventually moved to Abbotsford.

In 2012, I expanded my skip-tracing agency and franchised with another company, I was with them for about 5 years, at which time I severed our business relationship, as it was really. not working for me.

Skip-tracing, is quite interesting. You see you get to work with a lot of people throughout the world and you get to talk to people and find people anywhere in the world. It is not limited to your local geographical area. I have had the wonderful experience reuniting two adult daughters with their father who they hadn't seen since they were two, and their father was 79. I have had the pleasure of reuniting a mother who gave eight children up for adoption. I have located people in Kenya, and the Turks and Caicos Islands. I have located people in Italy.

I have reunited people who have been separated by adoption. When you work cases like I do, you love to see the positivity of your work. Transitioning to becoming a private investigator, initially was a dream. How it started, was browsing Craigslist, one day, and I saw an advertisement stating Private Investigator looking for information regarding the Highway of Tears. At this time I was residing in an apartment and my neighbour had disclosed he had been criminally convicted of murder, in the nineties, and that he had killed a female prostitute in the downtown east side of Vancouver. I looked into my neighbour and checked the court services online website which is a website that listed traffic and criminal offences in British Columbia. On this website I saw that my neighbour had multiple traffic tickets along the Highway of Tears, around the same time women were going missing.

So due to him being a neighbour, and an immediate one to say the least, I decided to respond to the Craigslist advertisement. I didn't of course want to use my own. name as I was concerned for the safety factors should my information be correct. I created a gmail account under the name Laura Goddard, and I responded to the advertisement. I advised in my email that it was a fake account, and that I was using a fake account because I was not certain if it was the killer themselves that was looking to witnesses, or if the poster of the advertisement truly was a private investigator, and I asked how one would verify that one was indeed a private investigator as they claimed. I received a response back from a man who identified himself as Lee Hanlon, at this time I did not put two and two together and had no idea that he was the same Lee Hanlon, whom I had dealt with on the Facebook Group in 2011.

We had several emails back and forth which led me to meeting him in person. During the multiple emails between Lee, and I, Lee, had suggested I become a private investigator, and even said that he had a referred me to a woman who was looking for a relative. A few days after this, I received a call from Security Programs Licensing division of Private Investigators advising me that they had received a complaint that I was running a private investigation agency without being licensed. I explained to the special constable that no I was not doing private investigation work that I was providing skip tracing services.

They closed their file on their investigation on me stating they don't regulate skip-tracing. Shortly after this, I decided I would apply for my private investigator license and in May of 2016, I received my private investigator license in the Province of British Columbia.

It was at this time on a Saturday, I received a call from a friend who was a private investigator whom I knew for over twenty years. He advised me that he received an email, from a Lee Hanlon, entitled "PI in British Columbia committing fraud.", In this email, Lee Hanlon, made a ton of allegations, stating that I was committing fraud, and that I conned my private investigator licensing body into giving me my license, that I had copied the services from my friends website and that I had no training to be a private investigator. He further went on to say that I had serious mental health issues etc. I filed a police report and police recommended charges against Lee, for Defamatory Libel. I proceeded to open my private investigator agency in July of 2016. It was at this point that I stopped communicating with Lee Hanlon, and wrote him a Cease and Desist letter advising him I wanted no contact with him. Again, I was looking at adverts on craigslist and saw multiple advertisements now naming my. newly licensed private investigation agency which would allude that I was a fraudulent company etc. These turned out to be placed online by Lee Hanlon.

I remember when I received my license and I told my mother about it. She was so excited for me, I finally had accomplished becoming a professional, working in a regulated industry. You see I grew up in foster care, I also have a diagnosed mental health issue, and I surpassed all of the obstacles and challenges along the way, and was able to achieve the career of my dreams.

I will always remember my first case. It was a domestic matter, and I was hired by a law firm as they were representing a client who had a child who they had being cared by relatives while the father was out of the country. My job was to determine whether or not the child was being cared for by a nanny or the paternal grandparents. This investigation took me into a casino as the subjects were consistently there spending thousands upon thousands of dollars at the Roulette table. Of course I couldn't just sit in the casino and not play anything or the security would wonder why I was there. I had been provided $50.00 to play with. I stretched this out over the course of like 7 hours. It worked, then I won about $100.00 (less the $50) so of course I provided that back to the client as in my opinion it would have been client funds as it was the clients $50.00 I was using to play to begin with. It was the most boring file one could work, especially if you don't believe in gambling as it is a waste of time and money.

I ended up getting the evidence I needed and provided it to the law firm. Transitioning from skip-tracing to conducting investigations was vastly different. Especially when you have a regulatory body to answer to. I found myself reading the legislation backwards and forwards to ensure I was in compliance. I didn't want to screw anything up for myself. If I had questions I was quick to get on the phone with my regulatory body, to ensure I was doing everything properly. I think this annoyed them, but hey if you are not sure its best to check, after all I didn't want to do anything that would jeopardize my licensing after I worked my ass off to get so far in my career. Before long,

I ended up taking the Security Training Course, so that I could work Loss Prevention, as I absolutely loved Loss Prevention. It was fun to walk the floor pretending to be a shopper and busting people who were stealing. Looking at me you would never think I was security. I am 5 foot 7, 164 lbs. I am also in my mid 40's. You would never think I was a private investigator let alone a loss prevention investigator. Plus I am female to boot, which stereotypically people think Loss Prevention Investigators are male, and private investigators are male. Boy are they wrong.

I find being a female in the Investigation Industry, has a ton of advantages. The transition to private investigation work went really smoothly, that is until Lee Hanlon, started his defamation against me. It is ironic given, that Lee Hanlon, was the one who informed me how to get a license, and why I should become a private investigator in the first place. I think this all started between him and I due to the fact I would not hire him in-house, as at the time he requested me to hire him I was not licensed as an agency, and stated that I could not provide the services until I was licensed accordingly as a business. I further informed him that I had. no requirement to hire him.

I think the other issue Lee Hanlon, had with me was that a) I was female and b) I wasn't required to do the 2000 training hours as a private investigator under supervision, as I had obtained my license through knowledge. Meanwhile, Lee Hanlon had counted down his hours of PI Under Supervision in his public Facebook profile. The other issue Lee Hanlon, had I believe was that I was a female, and he has issues with people who have a mental health diagnosis. Regardless, of what Lee Hanlon's presumed issues with me were what he did to me was not okay in any way, and was completely unwarranted.

~ Three ~

"ONLINE - REAL LIFE COLLIDE"

When I am bored, I tend to read advertisements on the website Craigslist.org. During such time, I found an advertisement of a private investigator wanting to obtain information about the missing women cases, which was dubbed as the Highway of Tears. The advertisement, did not really disclose who the poster was or provide their identity. It could have been anyone that had posted the advertisement.

At this time I was living in a high rise apartment on the eleventh floor, and I had a neighbour, who had disclosed to me he was a truck driver, and that he had spent time incarcerated in Ontario, Canada for murder, as well that he had been additionally charged with murder for killing a female indigenous prostitute in the Vancouver, downtown east side. I looked my neighbour up on the Court Services Online website, a database which shows criminal and civil case files throughout BC. I found that my neighbour had extensive traffic tickets all along Highway 16 which was dubbed as Highway of Tears, because women would go missing along the highway.

I emailed the advertisement, under the assumed name "Laura Goddard", and told the poster that I was emailing under such, as I did not know if the poster was the killer themselves looking for witnesses, or if they truly were a private investigator as the ad stated. You never know who it is behind any advertisement posted online. It virtually could be anyone. I wanted to ensure that I knew who the poster was prior to divulging the information I wished to share, as well as to confirm who the poster was, as my response to the advertisement could really assist in the investigation that the poster was looking for information on.

E-mail Response to Craigslist Advertisement
Author, Jolene Johnson

A few hours later after my email was sent I received a response from the email account, with a male identified himself as being "Lee Hanlon". He had stated he was a private investigator, and at this time I had not put two and two together quite yet.

The next day, I received an email from Lee Hanlon, through my website www.nationalpeoplelocator.com. In this email, Lee Hanlon, had started critiquing my website, although really my website had absolutely nothing to do with him. I responded thanking him, and he continued to make statements about my website. At this time, I was not a private investigator, and I really did not care for his input.

In the email Lee Hanlon, sent me was one that he was advising what I could and could not do on my website. He was trying to tell me I was contravening the Security Service Act, yet at this time I was not a private investigator and I was solely providing skip-tracing services, which I had been for over twenty years. I did not even think that this guy was the same guy that I had the brief encounter with in 2011. But, then that brief contact really was not something that one would remember, given it had no significant meeting to me. If only I had been able to put two and two together.

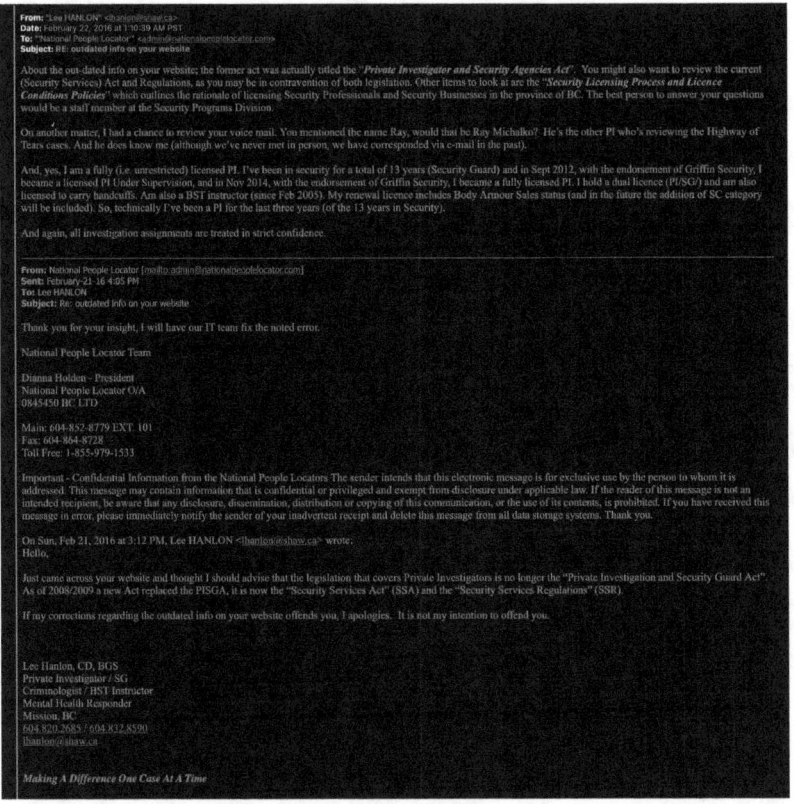

E-mail received by the Author Regarding Website from Lee Hanlon February 2016

Shortly, after receiving this email correspondence, I received a call from a Special Constable, with the Security Programs division of the Ministry of Solicitor General, the regulatory body for private investigators and security workers, informing me that they were conducting an investigation into my skip-tracing agency, as they needed to confirm that I was not running a private investigation agency without the proper licensing. This investigation was stemmed by a public complaint. I spoke with the special constable, and they ruled that the report was unfounded, and that they do not regulate skip-tracing.

On February 28, 2016, Lee Hanlon had sent me an email wanting me to know that he had provided my name as a referral for an adoption case. I really thought this was odd, given I barely knew the man and he knew nothing about my skip-tracing agency, or my abilities to locate people.

Moving forward to March 18, 2016, I received yet another email from Lee Hanlon, advising that he had went through notes and recalled me from being a part of a Facebook group, and he stated that people were making allegations against him that he was a worker working for MCFD, the local child protection agency in British Columbia. On the same day, I received yet another email to which he attached a copy of his resume and his Security Worker license and asked if I would hire him as a Private Investigator.

I continued to receive emails from him, and on April 3, 2016, Lee sent me a long winded email, asking me if I wanted to become a Private Investigator. He further suggested that I hire him as a PI, as well as wanted me to open a PI Training School.

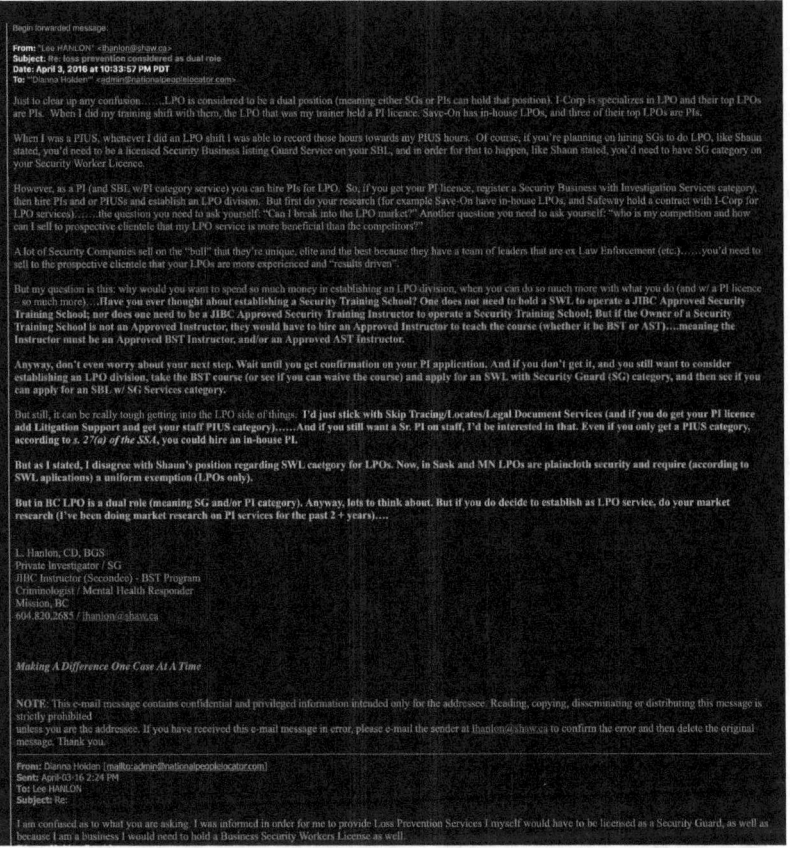

E-mail from Hanlon wanting to be hired April 3, 2016

Throughout February, March and the early weeks of April 2016, Lee Hanlon, continued to email me, his emails were written that of someone who was a colleague. Although, we had no relationship whatsoever, and we did not work together.

On April 10th, the emails even became stranger as now he was emailing advising me of a marketing person he knew. In fact asked me if I would use them and if so to advise them that I received their name from him. At this point we had never met. He advised me he had issues with a laptop he had as he was looking for a charging cable for it. I advised that I had an additional one. We agreed to meet in person. The next day, this short bald headed man arrives wearing a very large suit which looked funny given his short stature. My boyfriend was home during this meeting. At the time, when I decided to meet him, my live-in boyfriend was home, and I still was not able to place Lee, as the person from 2011, that I had issues with. Wanting to help him out he came over and I gave him the laptop charging cable. He was visiting with my boyfriend and I, for about ten minutes when there was a incident outside. Lee took off went flying to his car, grabbed something and raced off across the street. Then next thing we know police are there, and he storms over to his own vehicle and drives away.

On April 17, 2016, I received yet another email from Lee Hanlon, asking if I was going to be able to provide him a formal / informal interview at my office. I respond by telling him that I cannot hire him, unless I am licensed. I further inform him that if I receive my PI license, I would bring him on, however I had to do everything according to the legislation.

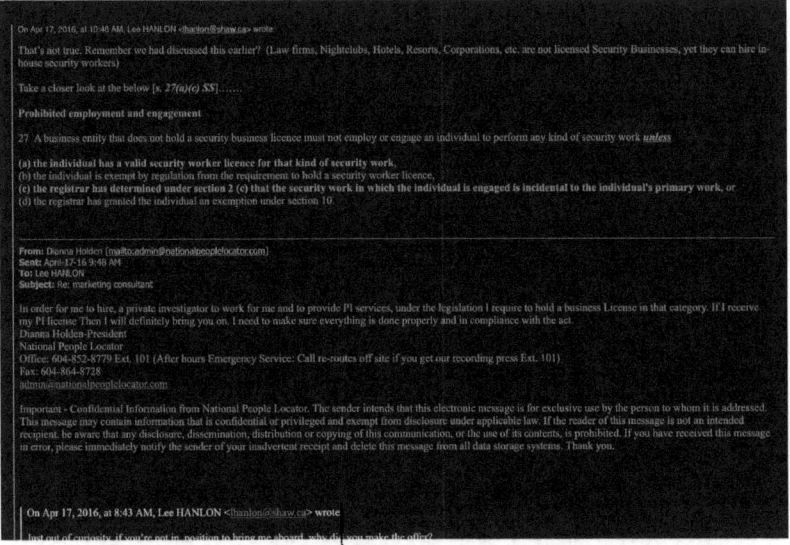

Hanlon E-mail stating I could hire him in-house April 17, 2016

I provided him the information and I also provided him the laptop charger cord. During this very brief meeting we stood on my balcony, and looked down at the road below, and observed two men fighting. After about being at my apartment for about ten minutes, Lee, ran out of my apartment went to his car and to retrieve his handcuffs, and bolted across the street. I then observed police attend, and Lee, left quickly and departed in his old nineties car.

A few more emails were sent to me by Lee Hanlon, and he asked me if he would be able to work for my skip-tracing agency as an in-house private investigator. I informed him that I did not require his services. We then discussed via email how he could tell me how to become a private investigator. He also offered to refer some lady to me to find someone. Lee, continued to email me wanting to work for me, which I politely declined. It was at this time I did apply for my private investigation license, and I became a private investigator May 2016.

Shortly, after I received my license I received an email from Lee Hanlon, (whom I didn't tell that I got my pi license to) asking me for a copy of my license stating that he just wanted to look at it. I stated that I had no reason to provide it to him as I was not working as I was not attached to a licensed security business, he then got irate with me as I refused to provide it to him. He continued to demand to see it and stated that I had too. I ignored these demands. In June of 2016, I opened up my agency NPL Services Inc. and. had it licensed as a private investigation agency. I was now an official Private Investigator, I was very happy and excited. Finally, my dreams were starting to come true. I was told that I would not amount to anything growing up, and now I could prove to people that it was nonsense and that you can be whatever you chose to be.

My excitement quickly diminished, when a colleague of mine emailed me advising that he had received an email stating that I was committing fraud, and that I had fraudulently obtained my private investigator license, and that I was mentally unstable and a con artist. I realized this was authored by no and behold Lee Hanlon. I immediately contacted the police, and I wrote him a Cease & Desist Letter advising him to stop. It was at this time he responded back stating that we had spoken in 2011, and it was now I realized that my online activity and real life had just collided. This was that stranger that messaged me, too which I had blocked on Facebook five years prior. This now was the beginning of crazy.

As I was reading other online advertisements, I came across ads about myself on the website LinkedIn, and Twitter. These advertisements were all under the user name "Lee Hanlon". I was being called a fraud, a liar, a terrible mother, and the list went on and on. I had to do something about this because it just was absolutely shocking that someone who didn't really know me would go to great lengths to try to destroy my reputation online. What was this mans goal, I really don't know although he must have needed some sort of professional help. As who in their right mind would harass virtually a stranger?

I thought long and hard and I really had to figure out what I was going to do. I decided I would go to the police, after all, they are there to help right? I also filed a complaint with my regulatory body, as there was no way they wouldn't do something about it. Of course that is what I thought, little did I know I was wrong and my regulatory body would do nothing to help.

~ Four ~

"THE POLICE INVESTIGATION"

Reporting a crime is challenging, mainly because you have to tell your story over and over again. You also, do not know what the outcome will be, and you are victimized all over again and have to relive the experience every time you tell your story. Then there is always the thought of what if they don't believe me.

I guess those are the thoughts that went through my head, solely because it just didn't seem real. Why on earth would an unknown "Private Investigator, start harassing me online and posting all kinds of false statements about me". It is not like I dated him, or knew him on a personal level. The thoughts that I wouldn't be believed, were common ones, as it just was so far fetched that someone who I truly did not have a personal relationship with what motive would they have to defame me, what vendetta would they truly have against me.?

I could not wrap my head around the fact that this was real. That some guy off of the internet would take it upon himself to post false statements about me, that he would take it upon himself to reach out to everyone known to me and lie about me.

It made absolutely no sense to me. I had never wronged him I didn't even know the guy.

I had to do something about what was going on. I couldn't just let it sit. The emotional impact his articles and statements that he was making about me online, started to take a toll on me. I decided, I would call the police. When I called, my file was assigned to a police officer who was very understanding and had compassion. This took me by surprise, after all, they were just words on the screen that I was complaining about. I was told that they would do an investigation.

Lee Hanlon, started writing about me on various sites, such as LinkedIn, Facebook, Twitter, Craigslist etc. It was as if every other day, he had something new to say about me. I thought to myself how on earth could a man have so much hatred towards someone who was never in any sort of relationship with them. I could see how someone could hate, if they were an ex husband, ex boyfriend, or even a disgruntled business partner. However, Lee, was none of this. We had no relationship this is what I found so scary and unsettling.

During the course of the police investigation, I started to receive several messages from prospective clients, only to find out that they were not clients at all, they were Lee Hanlon, messaging me under an assumed identity, to harass me. He would email me stating he needed surveillance by aircraft, or by boat. It came to light it was Lee posting this, as he admitted it to one of my staff to which he was in frequent contact with. Why Lee, had decided to speak to any of my staff is beyond me. Regularly I would be asked who Lee, was as they were getting messages from him and they don't know him. I was being told that he was asking questions about me to them. He would contact my mother, who also didn't know who he was or why he would be contacting her.

The articles he was posting was creating havoc for my work. Especially, when I was trying to locate people, they would do a google of my name and up would pop up Lee Hanlon's articles about me. Regardless, the fact that they were not containing truthful facts, the damage was done. Lee, would post things about my personal medical information which I had the right to privacy. Lee, managed to destroy my entire business and personal character. You see clients don't want to take a chance when they google someone, they would rather retain someone who has no dirt drudged up on the internet. Clients do not look to see if statements made are true or not, if they find something at all they hire someone else who has nothing. This is why it affected my business to the extent it did. As well, when I would continue skip-tracing people would google me and see the articles and then draw my attention to them.

When I would try to get a contract they would google and see the same shit. It was next to impossible to continue obtaining clientele. I was also having difficulties hiring people because they as well would google and find the defamatory articles written about me.

I had two police officers attend my residence, and take a statement from me. I later found out that the police also took statements from employees who worked for me, and others as well. Throughout the entire police investigation, more articles were popping up. Pretty soon the google searches started to be just negative about me. It was near Christmas, and I was told that the police were recommending charges against Lee Hanlon. They were recommending he be charged with publishing libel known to be false under s. 300 of the Criminal Code of Canada.

Great now I was starting to feel hopeful that this all would stop. Thinking that finally the police are taking this seriously, I truly believed that Lee Hanlon, would stop being a keyboard warrior. I truly thought he would move on to something more productive. Unfortunately, it did not pan out that way because in January, I got word that the crown prosecutor, decided to not charge him, claiming it was not in the public interest.

You see Crown Counsel, has to approve charges against someone, and they have a charge approval process, which means if they feel that it is not in the Public Interest they will not proceed. In this case, they felt it was not a matter of public interest and dropped it all. Leaving me with no justice. I felt like my heart had been ripped out of my body. How could it not be a public interest matter. After all, he was a licensed private investigator, he worked with the public daily, and with vulnerable people, but yet they said not public interest. I did not get their charge approval process as it seemed very flawed. If Crown Counsel, refuses to charge someone there is really nothing you can do about it.

Really, my world was crashing down on me again. Why was it not in the Public Interest? The guy was a licensed private investigator, by now I had found out he was contacting my employees, he was talking about me in hidden group chats on Facebook, and they stated it was not in the public interest. I decided to file a complaint with Security Programs, they denied my complaint stating he was working in a personal capacity and not that of a security worker. Justice denied there too.

I had no options left, but to talk to a lawyer and sue him. Lee Hanlon, continued to contact my staff, he would contact my secretary, he would contact my skip-tracers. Throughout all of his contacts he would state that he was a private investigator, and that he was investigating me. He even contacted one of my staff who was in charge of my marketing. His fascination with me was of the upmost concern. The police continued to monitor the Facebook posts that were being posted, and the articles, and gathered tons of evidence. Crown would not have any of it, they would not charge him.

Once again the system failed me. This seems to be a common occurrence when it comes to when I make a complaint. I felt angry and hurt, and although I had never posted anything in retaliation against Lee, I still could not fathom why the prosecutors office took the stance they did. It most definitely was in the public interest. You see Lee Hanlon, posted about others too, it was not just myself. Anytime, Lee, didn't like someone, or felt he was wronged, he would become this keyboard warrior. Soon his time would be up, soon he would be put in his place. I decided the best way to do this, and to get him to stop, is to file a lawsuit so off to the lawyers I went. I soon began to realize there is no justice.

~ Five ~

COMMENCING LITIGATION

Some people will say that I am litigious. I can honestly say, at times in order to obtain justice, people are left with the only option as to sue. Throughout my life, I have had to sue people for a variety of reasons. Being harassed online and defamed by a Private Investigator, certainly was one of these times. In order, to obtain an order to remove defamatory content off of the internet, you have to commence a law suit. Unfortunately, there was no other way to obtain this order. So on August 8, 2017, I retained a lawyer and filed a suit against Lee Hanlon, for Defamation.

When you are left with no alternative, but to engage a civil suit, because everything else fails, it again takes an emotional toll on your wellbeing. I still did not know why I was the target of Lee Hanlon. Was it because he wanted employment with me and I failed to hire him, was there some underlying issue that created his strong distaste for me? Was he secretly obsessed with me as I was a woman? Only he can answer these questions. I always wondered how we went from simple conversations through email, at the time which I truly did not connect him to the earlier Facebook conversations in 2011.

Lee, would email me and give me advice on opening a private investigation and security company. He even said he would work for me in-house as a private investigator. It was not until I informed him, that I could not hire him until my business NPL Services, was adequately licensed that I would be able to hire him, he did an about face, and changed his tune becoming very abusive through email. I started to notice a change in Lee, specifically when it came to his online persona. One minute he was emailing me stating he had provided a referral for me to locate someone's relative, and the next he was saying that I could hire an internal private investigator without being licensed as an agency.

The minute I would disagree with his prospective, he would start using vulgarity in the email and get upset. The funny thing is that initially I was going to work with him, because what I saw was a diamond in the ruff. Yes Lee had his corks, but who doesn't? I guess I see the abilities rather than the disabilities. I like to see the good in people. Deep down I thought that Lee, just had some very strong views, and had a fluctuation in moods, I truly thought it was due to all the rejection that he faced throughout his life. I truly thought we were so much alike.

People probably think that I am crazy saying nice things about a man who harassed me for so long online, but I really have never held any animosity against him. Don't get me wrong what he did really affected me, it rocked me to the core, but I still had compassion. I truly have never understood Lee's, attitude towards me, and I maybe never will. I always pictured sitting down with Lee, before the litigation was filed, and actually talking about what was bothering him. What was it that irked him so much about me? Was it that I was a female, was it that deep down he liked me but didn't want to admit it? Was it that he had a secret crush on me? You know in elementary school when boys pick on you it is truly because they like you. Well I have often wondered if this was the case with Lee Hanlon. Don't get me wrong, I absolutely have no interest in him not romantically or other, but I have always felt empathy and compassion for him. I guess this is truly why I never reciprocated any of the actions. he did towards me.

It was how I coped with the harassment for so long. If I didn't have compassion, or empathy for him I may have done something that I would have regretted. The compassion and empathy for Lee, was what kept me level headed. I truly did not want to lower myself to his level. I guess some didn't quite understand how I could keep a level head, How was it that I truly didn't express my anger towards him. I was extremely angry, but if I acted out with that anger, it truly wouldn't have got me anywhere I would be as low as him. I didn't want to provide any ammunition for it to be thought of a tit for tat situation. I didn't want Lee to know that deep down he hurt me to the core, but I would never admit it. After all if I did admit it, then he would view it as winning.

I always felt that there had to be a reason for the actions Lee did towards me. I don't think I will ever figure that one out. On August 8, 2017, I filed a litigation suit against Lee Hanlon, for Defamation. On October 5, 2017, I was granted a temporary injunction against him prohibiting him from continuing to post defamatory statements.

No. S-177572
Vancouver Registry

IN THE SUPREME COURT OF BRITISH COLUMBIA

Between:

Dianna Leigh Holden, NPL Services Inc. and National People Locator

Plaintiffs

And:

Lee Hanlon, Patricia Pelley, Lorelei Rochelle Edwards, Facebook Inc., Google Inc., Her Majesty the Queen in Right of British Columbia as represented by the Assistant Deputy Attorney General, Criminal Justice Branch and Vincent Schmele

Defendants

ORDER MADE AFTER APPLICATION

BEFORE) THE HONOURABLE JUSTICE SEWELL) 05/Oct/2017

On the application of Dianna Holden and NPL Services Inc coming on for hearing at Vancouver, British Columbia on October 5, 2017, and on hearing Todd Brayer, counsel for the Plaintiffs, Stephanie Lacuesta, for Her Majesty the Queen in Right of British Columbia as represented by the Assistant Deputy Attorney General, Criminal Justice Branch and Lee Hanlon, personally.

THIS COURT ORDERS:

1. Lee Hanlon ("**Hanlon**") or any agent of Hanlon's SHALL BE ENJOINED FROM either directly or indirectly, writing, publishing, posting or in any way distributing or making public any accusatory or disparaging allegations regarding the honesty, trustworthiness or alleged improper behaviour of Dianna Holden ("**Holden**"), NPL Services Inc. ("**NPL**") and National People Locator in any forum of any kind whatsoever and enjoining Hanlon from directing or assisting others in writing, publishing posting to the Internet or in any way distributing or making public such allegations until further order of the Court;

2. Within 48 hours of the date of this order, Hanlon shall remove all publications he has made on the Internet or websites including but not limited to Craigslist.com, Facebook.com ("**Facebook**"), Listedhs.com ("**Lisedslls**").

Interim Injunction October 2017

Brainsyntax.com ("**Brainsyntax**") and Securusresearch.wixsite.com/mysite ("**Hanlon's Personal Website**") respecting Holden, NPL and Nationas People Locator including, but not limited to the following postings:

a. Posting dated July 8, 2016 on Craigslist entitled "SCAM ALERT: NPL SERVICES INC";

b. All postings made on the Facebook group "United Victims of Dianna Holden";

c. Posting in September 2016 on Facebook group titled "WTF Abbotsford" respecting Holden;

d. Posting made in October 2016 titled "Charter of Rights Freedom of Speech Under Attack", that was either edited or reposted on December 25, 2016.

e. Posting made on or around May 14, 2017 on the Facebook group "Veterans Transition Network";

f. Posting dated August 7, 2017 titled "Beware of PI Con-Artists";

g. Posting dated August 21, 2017 titled "Freedom of Speech Under Attack";

h. Posting dated August 26, 2017 on the Facebook group "Canada Court Watch";

i. Posting dated September 4, 2017 titled "Intimidation Tactics by Dianna Holden";

j. Posting dated September 10, 2017 titled "Criminal Harassment (AKA Stalking) Laws in Canada"; and

k. Various posts on Facebook, Brainsyntax and elsewhere respecting Holden and NPL;

3. The Plaintiffs shall provide an undertaking to Hanlon as to damages pursuant to Rule 10-4(5) of the *Supreme Court Civil Rules* to abide by any order that the court may make as to damages.

4. The requirement of Hanlon to sign this order is hereby dispensed with; and

5. Costs will be in the cause.

APPROVED AS TO FORM

_____
Todd Brayer
Counsel for the Plaintiffs

_____
Stephanie Lacuesta
Counsel for Her Majesty the Queen in Right of British Columbia as represented by the Assistant Deputy Attorney General, Criminal Justice Branch

By the Court

_____
Registrar

With the injunction, it was very clear that the overwhelming amount of articles posted about me were not only disturbing but were also meant to defame me. This was not just a simple case of someone who had a relationship with someone and was scorned. It was an individual who truly had a distaste for me, which was very disturbing given I had no relationship with him on a personal level, nor did I have a professional relationship with him. At the time that Lee, started this vicious campaign against me, I had only met him briefly for ten minutes.

I ended up naming other parties because they colluded with him. Going through life at times you befriend the wrong person, or end up with a client that has their own issues, such as Lorelei, and Patricia Pelley. This was the beginning of the litigation. You see, the internet can be a really good thing, that is if there is some regulation to what people post. When you use the internet as a forum to create havoc, and post untruthful things, well that is an entirely different story.

Now that I had the injunction, one would would think this entire saga would end. No it certainly did not. Lee, would continue to post etc. and it certainly did not stop him. Lee, would contact everyone known to me to try to get people to listen to him spew his filth about me. He continued to message my staff he continued to try to get people to send stuff to him from my business. In fact he upped his game, by contacting my staff once again. Only this time the staff member he approached, would turn against me, and testify at the trial.

Within days of obtaining the injunction, Lee Hanlon, breached it. Unfortunately, the same conduct continued. There were posts online and more. Only this time he was a little more secretive, he would private message people through different platforms, he would physically speak to people about me discussing the same old theme of how much. he thought I was a criminal a fraud and a con-artist. None of what he was spewing was true.

I. had to write many Affidavits for my lawyer, and lay out all the facts as I knew them. I had to scour the internet for days on end to capture all of the posts that he had posted in order to have them removed. I had to constantly watch the shit. he was posting to ensure that he was not posting my address etc. which could inadvertently cause a safety issue for myself and my children. It was a very daunting task, as it was not as easy as just shutting off the computer and walking away. I had to know what was being posted because I did not know much about him, and I needed to stay safe.

Litigation can take years. Not only does it take time but it is a very gruelling process and it definitely not easy to navigate without having a lawyer. Even after I served Lee, with our civil action he would continue his rampage. Nothing was stopping him not even the law suit. Although I had an injunction (court order prohibiting him from continuing) it costs money to hold one in contempt of court. They are not easy to obtain. So really, he was getting away with everything. We went through a summary trial, this is a fast track trial which is done strictly by written submissions. We did a three day summary trial to which the judge ruled that it needs to go to a full trial. Off we went to a full trial.

~ Six ~

WHO IS LEE HANLON?

One would wonder who Lee Hanlon, is. Various websites have articles he has written, telling of many stories from failed relationships and marriages, to growing up with an abusive father named Walter Franks. Lee Hanlon, was consistently posting on his Facebook of about how his father was abusive to him at a young age. It is truly difficult to decipher whether what is written by Lee Hanlon, has any truth to it as when he defamed me I can certainly say there was no substance to any of the allegations he made about me.

What one can only assume from his lengthly list of self-proclaimed employment adventures, to his multiple writings that discuss a fascination with the missing women along the Highway of Tears, later changed to Highway of Heroes, to the human trafficking and family justice sites he is a part of. Lee Hanlon, craves for attention, and wants to feel important. He needs to feel important.

Lee Hanlon, was not always Lee Hanlon. You see he was born under the name of Martello Leroi Franks, and completed a legal name change. The reasons he changed his name are not really clear. Looking at Lee Hanlon's profiles on the internet you will see that he claims he has been a seventeen year veteran. What we do know is that he was a reservist with the Canadian Department of National Defence. The amount of time he spent as a reservist remains to be seen. However, he writes articles about how he was bullied in the military, and that they discharged him due to allegations an ex-wife had made pertaining to him. The bottom line, is Lee Hanlon, is an individual who does not think before he posts online, he can be nice to you one minute and a nightmare the next. I found anytime I thought differently than he did he would go on the personal attack towards me.

Lee, also has informed people he has a black belt in Karate. You would think one who has the extensive stamina and training to obtain that level of belt in Karate, that they would be more posed, and have a level head.

Lee likes to roller-skate in the USA, in fact prior to the pandemic he would attend the USA every other weekend and roller-skate. Even at the age of 61. Why a 61 year old would feel the need to attend a roller rink, remains to be seen.

Lee has many fascinations, specifically with anything to do with Law Enforcement. He applied for the Royal Canadian Mounted Police, and his application as a police officer was denied. He applied to be a Transit Police Officer, he was denied, He applied for Abbotsford City Police Department, he was denied. So he decided to become a private investigator, as his career dreams of being a police officer were unsuccessful. Lee, claims he was a first year law student, and in fact the Law Society of British Columbia, had to obtain a court order preventing him from practising law without a license to practice law, in 2002.

Lee lives in the basement of his mothers home in Mission, British Columbia. As of the writing of this publication he states he pays no rent. There is not a lot to be said about Lee Hanlon, himself, a quick google search of his name will provide you multitudes of links of his personal writings which all seem to be surrounding terrorism, Judaism, missing women etc. It appears from reviewing his extensive articles, that he has a large variety of opinions about a multitude of issues.

Throughout Lee's life, he has made it known he feels like a victim. He feels that people are cyberstalking him, and that they are the problem. Lee, from his writings never seems to be accountable for what his part is in anything he does. Its rather disturbing, to say the least.

I remember when I first physically met Lee, although the meeting was all of about 10 minutes, in length, he had popped by my apartment when my boyfriend was home to pick up a lap top charger cord. At this time Lee and I were cordial with one another. I didn't have any reason to think the man would defame me for years to come. When I met him, he seemed really nice, very professional, but I remember sitting outside on my eleventh storey balcony and Lee, was terrified of heights and wouldn't come out.

While I was sitting out on the balcony there was a drug deal that went bad outside on the ground below us, Lee, took off like a wild man, stopping at his car, selected his handcuffs out of his car and I could see him running over to the strip mall across. Shortly after I observed police attend and it appeared they told him to scramble and I watched him walk back to his car and depart.

Observing this altercation, surprised me that he would get involved he wasn't law enforcement and really had no reason to become involved in this type of issue. It did present that he was a police officer wannabe, in my opinion. The scary part of it all, is a private investigator really has no power, meaning we do not have access to special databases, we do not have any police powers etc. and here is Lee Hanlon, trying to assert power he truly does not have.

When you physically meet Lee, you will see that he is a very quiet little man, with a bald head, and appears to not be very confident. Intellectually, he comes across as a very smart individual hell how can you pretend to be a lawyer when you're not? That takes guts and smarts. When I would talk with him he would keep throwing legislation at you of the private investigation licensing act, yet he would misconstrue the meaning of the act. This was a concern, for me and one of the reasons why I had decided to not hire him.

The other reason I had chosen not to hire him was due to the vulgarity he used in his email correspondence to me. He appeared to be very unpredictable. I felt he just was not the right fit with my agency.

~ Seven ~

THE TRIAL

The morning of the Defamation trial, I was nervous. I woke up thinking god is this really happening. What exactly is going to occur. I had been inside a court room before briefly only on the defence side. I won that case so I knew my lawyer well, and knew he was an excellent lawyer. I guess that is why I hired the same lawyer to do my defamation case. I arrive at the court house with my entourage, comprised of my legal team, a personal friend, and an employee of my company.

I was not really sure how Supreme Court would work out, as I had only been in Provincial Court prior. So it's the morning of August 7 and we all arrive at the courthouse. I am dressed business casual, my legal team of course have their lawyer gowns on. In walks Lee Hanlon, wearing the most funniest suit ever. Picture a very short bald man, wearing suit pants that are about four inches too long, carrying a very tattered black briefcase. Truly, I felt sorry for the guy, he reminded me of the character Mini-me, played by Verne Troyer, in the movie Austin Powers. Lee, walked up to the table in front of the court room, and I had to sit in the gallery, as I hand counsel, and Lee, was self-represented.

The beginning of the trial, I found very overwhelming and boring to say the least. I would sit there intently listening to my lawyers give their opening speeches, I would listen to the judge presiding over the matter and observe her body language. I was observing Lee, and listening to what he was saying and writing notes on my notepad to provide to my lawyers should the need arise. When people say watching court trials is interesting, they are boring, even when you are a part of the proceeding. The first day was taxing for me emotionally. Not only did I need to relive all of the nasty comments and allegations Lee, had written online about me, now I had to listen to them be to to a judge who would be deciding whether or not he posted defamatory comments. I thought to myself is she going to think of myself as a lesser person, even though all of the shit Lee, posted was false. I thought about how anyone could come bursting through the court room door and listen to this. At times I found it so difficult to bite my tongue especially when Lee, started spouting off lie after lie. (The lie's I am referring to are the repeating of the defamatory statements.).

Then the unexpected happened. I saw one of my former staff members Olivia Hanson, and her boyfriend in the court gallery. They were also my immediate neighbours. Prior to my legal counsel presenting my case, the judge allowed Lee Hanlon, to have his first witness. Olivia Hanson, took the stand. On the stand in a nutshell she testifies that I was committing identity theft, that I was misrepresenting myself as Amazon, etc, to obtain people's addresses. This was completely false. She goes on to tell the court that she is a Whistleblower, and that she had stolen thousands of documents from my office and provided them to Lee Hanlon. She tells the court that she worked for me as a marketer, and head of sales. She further testifies that I would join the sales calls and advise potential clients that I had been subjected to defamation. Further testimony was that I used a Credit Scoring website to obtain people's credit scores. Other testimony was that I was trying to frame Lee Hanlon, by creating false accounts making it look like he was practicing law without a license (remember he was taken to court by the Law Society of British Columbia for practicing law without being a licensed lawyer). According to the judge, she ruled that Olivia Hanson, was a disgruntled employee. After all she did testify that she stole tons of documents from my office and just gave them to Lee Hanlon.

While she was testifying, one would think her body language would indicate that she was nervous. After all if she was nervous she should have been. She was sitting up there lying about me. Let me tell you a bit about Olivia. Firstly, she was my next door neighbour, prior to commencing work at my office. I had established a friendship sorta. She had previously worked at a large retail store in sales. She had left this position because of what she alleged as workplace harassment because she was transgender, and had changed her birth sex of male to female. Looking at Olivia, you would see long straight red hair, she was about 5 foot 10. She still had some masculine features, as she was still in the process of changing, and was on hormone replacement. When I looked at her, you could barely tell she had previously been a male. I remember one time she came over onto my back deck. Her and her boyfriend Rowan, who also was transgender and was born female, had a fight. Olivia, suffered panic attacks, and severe panic attacks. I remember one day I came home and found Olivia on my back deck curled up in a ball crying and rocking back and forth. I ended up getting Rowan's mom to come over because I really didn't know what to do. I had never seen anyone present this way while having a panic attack.

    We got her through it. She then went home. Olivia would come over to my house regularly. She was a really nice person and had amazing IT skills, and doubled in my admin department handling all of our websites, social media, email accounts, she would show us different websites we could use for finding people. She was an amazing employee. Why she decided to testify at the trial I still to this day do not understand. She also was afraid of going out and severe anxiety around people. Olivia, also suffered with depression, and Rowan would also come over and tell me how he had found her in the basement sticking a bag over her head or sometimes she would try to strangle herself with the sash from. her housecoat. I wonder if it was the hormones she was taking that made her this way.

    Olivia, had said she grew up in a very religious family. Her parents were one of Jehovah's Witnesses. Once she transitioned, her mother had disowned her. I spoke to Olivia's mother at her request because she longed for a relationship with her mother, but it didn't fair well, as her mother refused to see Olivia as a woman and kept misgendering her. Therefore, the relationship just would not work, at least that is what Olivia shared with me.

    To watch her up on the stand was like watching a bad movie. I was watching this woman who I had compassion for, and who I liked as a person, turn into an evil monster and spew lies from her mouth. When it came time for my lawyer to cross examine her, there really wasn't much to say. Olivia, admitted to stealing thousands of documents and emails from my office, and tried to justify her actions by stating she was a whistle blower, and also stated that she gave them to Lee Hanlon, because we didn't.

Olivia, felt that it was truly okay to steal from her employer. Her testimony was short, and in the judges decision the judge ruled she was completely not credible and was just a disgruntled employee. The judge got it right!.

Now it was my turn to take the stand. I had to go through every article, every statement that Lee Hanlon, posted about me and explain my version of the events and why the statements were not true. It was a very daunting task. It was a very gruelling process to be under a microscope although you are guilty of nothing. Upon my lawyer presenting my evidence, it was now Lee Hanlon's turn, who was playing lawyer in his own case to cross examine me. The cross examination took place like this:

> Q Ms. Holden, is it true you're a debt -- a licenced debt collector?
> A Yes, that is true.
> Q Okay.
> THE COURT: And, Mr. Hanlon, I know that it's difficult to go slowly, but you want me to take notes, so --
> LEE HANLON: Yes, My Lady.
> THE COURT: -- if you could just go slowly.
> LEE HANLON:
> Q And as a debt collector you have authorization to access credit bureau information?
> A Depends on the file, yes.
> Q And the type of file would be a skip trace file only?
> A No, it would be a file that's listed for debt collection.
> Q Do you also include files that are investigation files, like for private investigators?

A No.
Q No?
THE COURT: Okay. Just wait until he finishes --
A Sorry.
THE COURT: -- the question.
LEE HANLON:
Q Is it true that (REDACTED) -- is that how you pronounce her name, (REDACTED)?
A I'm not sure how to pronounce it.
Q Okay. It's spelled --
LEE HANLON: My Lady, it's -- last name is (REDACTED) First name is spelled (REDACTED)
Q Is it true that Ms. (REDACTED) was an investigation file?
A No.
THE COURT: Is what? I'm sorry. I didn't hear that.
LEE HANLON: An investigation file. Like, a file only a private investigator can do.
A No.
THE COURT: I don't know what (REDACTED) is.
LEE HANLON:
Q Oh, that's the name of the -- (REDACTED)is the name of the -- (REDACTED) is the name of the victim in the Credit Karma matter that Ms. Hanson brought up in the -- her testimony yesterday.
A No.
Q Isn't it correct that you were audited by Canada Revenue Agency?
A Yes, that's correct.
Q And is it correct that they assessed that you owe them $40,000?
A I don't know what the assessment was.

Q Okay. And they didn't tell you?
A I have not received any paperwork, no.
Q Okay. Thank you.
LEE HANLON: That's all for -- that's all my crossexamination, My Lady. I don't see any further -- everything else I can put in when I'm doing evidence.
THE COURT: You have no further questions?
LEE HANLON: No.
THE COURT: I am going to remind you, I said this in my outline, that if you're going to contradict the witness you need to put that to her.
LEE HANLON: Yes, My Lady.
THE COURT: You understand that?
LEE HANLON: Yes.
THE COURT: That's an important practice in our courts because otherwise she doesn't have an opportunity to respond.
LEE HANLON: Correct. Okay.
Q Is it true that -- is it correct that Constable Dionne [phonetic] of Mission RCMP contacted --
LEE HANLON: My apologies, My Lady.
Q Is it correct that Constable Dionne of the Mission RCMP contacted you?
A Yes.
Q Okay. And is it correct that she cautioned you regarding a cyber stalking investigation?
A No, she did not.
Q Did she caution you on a criminal harassment investigation?
A No, she did not.
Q Okay. Is it correct that Constable Williams of

the Wood Buffalo RCMP in Alberta contacted you?
A I don't know what you're referring to.
Q Okay. Is it correct as Laura Goddard you put out there that I could be a killer; correct?
A No, I did not.
Q Okay. Is it correct that your security guard category has been revoked?
A That is not correct.
Q Okay. Is it correct that you're under investigation for that possibly happen?
A No, that is not correct.
Q Is it correct that you are in the process of changing your name?
A I already have changed my name.
Q Okay. To -- okay. Thank you. And is it correct that on a phone recording that you instructed Ms. Hanson to do what's referred to as remote access?
A No, I've never allowed Ms. Hanson to have remote access to my computer.
Q So you never said anything on a telephone recording?
A No, I did not.
Q Okay. Would you be surprised if -- if you were told that the RCMP have a copy of that recording?
A That's what I heard in Ms. Hanson's evidence yesterday.
Q Okay. In December of 2011 is it correct that you accused me of being a private investigator for the Ministry of Children and Family Development?
A I did not accuse you of that. I stated that you were possibly working with them because you seemed to know a lot of information about me and I didn't

know you, and you randomly messaged me.
Q Okay. Is it correct that you made a statement in the correspondence that there was a mysterious girl that I dated that was in that group said that to you?
A I don't recall.
Q Okay. Isn't it correct that your employees have left you because you either paid them late or don't pay the at all?
A I don't know what their reasons are for leaving. Sometimes I terminate. Sometimes people quit.
Q Okay. Isn't it correct that in an email that's in my affidavit that was in the summary trial that you accused me of sabotaging your contract with Mark's Work Wearhouse?
A I did not.
MR. BRAYER: Do you have a copy of that email?
LEE HANLON: I do. Just one moment, My Lady.
THE COURT: Yes, that's fine. Did you find it, sir?
LEE HANLON: I'm just about there, My Lady. It's at my tab 16. My copy is marked, so I'm just going to get a copy from this one here that's not marked.
Q This email was dated September 7th, and it was sent --
THE COURT: What year, sir?
LEE HANLON: Oh, 2017.
THE COURT: And it's -- you've got a copy for counsel and the court?
LEE HANLON: It's in -- it's in my evidence in my binder, and I can give him -- I can give him this binder.

THE COURT: Sir -- counsel, do you have a copy? Because --

MR. BRAYER: I didn't find one on my computer, my laptop.

THE COURT: It's an email between whom and whom?

LEE HANLON: This is an email from Ms. Holden to myself.

THE COURT: All right. I just think it would -- it's not in the exhibit 5?

LEE HANLON: Not yet. We don't have a joint book of documents.

THE COURT: So you're going -- all right. Counsel, I think the best thing to do is if we just take a very quick recess and make copies of that.

MR. BRAYER: Very good.

THE COURT: So we're all off the same page. Mr. Registrar, if you could obtain the document, and we'll make copies.

THE CLERK: Yes, My Lady.

THE COURT: All right. We'll just take a very brief recess.

(WITNESS STOOD DOWN)

LEE HANLON: It's at the bottom of this first page, My Lady.

THE COURT: Yeah. So just refer --

LEE HANLON: Yes.

THE COURT: -- for the record this is an email from yourself to NPL Services dated September 7, 2017.

LEE HANLON: The other way around -- sorry. The other way around, My Lady. It's from NPL Services to myself.

THE COURT: But that's the bottom one.

LEE HANLON: At the bottom one. That's the bottom one I'm referring to.
THE COURT: And the witness has a copy?
A No, I don't, My Lady.
THE COURT: So put that before the witness.
CROSS-EXAMINATION BY LEE HANLON, CONTINUING:
Q So before --
THE COURT: So let -- just give her a moment to read it, please.
LEE HANLON: Yes, My Lady.
A I'm familiar with this email, My Lady.
THE COURT: What's your question, sir?
LEE HANLON:
Q So a few minutes ago before we stood down, I asked you if you accused me of sabotaging the contract with Mark's, and you said no, you did not. Okay. And this email it says -- or you're accusing me of sabotaging the email -- the -- sorry. You're accusing me of sabotaging the --
A I never stated that you sabotaged it. I stated that I was aware that you had been in contact with Mark's during the course of my contract with them, and it was making it very difficult for me to work at Mark's because of statements that were being made.
Q So is it true that you accused me of approaching your guard, one of your guards, while you had the contract at Mark's?
A Where are you looking at?
Q Same email. Same email.
A Whereabouts in the email, Mr. Hanlon?
Q Right underneath the "Dear, Mr. Hanlon." It

says
[as read in]:
You approached our uniformed guards who were working at the location on Saturday and made libel statements about me which led this guard to walking off his shift two hours in.
A Yes, I'm aware of that.
Q Okay.
A I was informed that by one of my static guards.
MR. BRAYER: Sorry. I don't see the relevance in any of this. There's no claim being made about anything that's in this email. The claim for defamation is very clearly set out in the notice of civil claim.
LEE HANLON:
Q Would it be a surprise to you, Ms. Holden, that I was never at that site while you had the contract?
A I don't know.
Q Okay.
LEE HANLON: I have no further questions, My Lady.

(WITNESS STOOD DOWN)

Throughout my time on the stand, I was curious as to what Lee, was going to ask next. I truly felt that he would just stop questioning me with all this nonsense and walk out of the court room in defeat, knowing that it was a huge facade. Of course he didn't. We finished the trial with Lee Hanlon providing evidence, and my lawyer cross examining him. The trial came to a close, and we had to wait for a year for the decision.

On April 23, 2019, Madam Justice Dardi, released her written decision. The synopsis of her decision was that Lee, had acted with Malice, and I was awarded $27,500.00 Unfortunately, right after the judgement was released, Lee, filed personal bankruptcy. Therefore, he didn't have to pay me a dime. I also received a permanent injunction which now reads like this:

[338] All things considered, I conclude that the totality of the evidence supports a finding that, in the absence of an injunction, there is a substantial likelihood that both defendants would continue to publish the defamatory statements. I conclude that a permanent injunction in the following term should be issued:

Lee Hanlon ("Hanlon"), any agent of Hanlon's, Vincent Schiele ("Schiele"), and any agent of Schiele, SHALL BE ENJOINED FROM either directly or indirectly, writing, publishing, posting or in any way distributing or making public any accusatory or disparaging allegations regarding the honesty, trustworthiness or alleged improper behaviour of Dianna Holden ("Holden"), NPL Services Inc. ("NPL") and National People Locator in any forum of any kind whatever and enjoining Hanlon and Schiele from directing or assisting others in writing, publishing, posting to the Internet or in any way distributing or making public such allegations and without limiting the generality of the foregoing, from posting allegations similar to those made in the following prior postings:

    a. Posting dated July 8, 2016 on Craigslist entitled "SCAM ALERT: NPL SERVICES INC.";

    b. All posting made on the Facebook group "United Victims of Dianna Holden";

    c. Posting in September 2016 on Facebook group titled "WTF Abbotsford" respecting Holden;

    d. Posting made in October 2016 titled "Charter of Rights Freedom of Speech Under Attack", that was either edited or reposted on December 25, 2016;

e. *Posting made on or around May 14, 2017 on the Facebook group "Veterans Transition Network";*

f. *Posting dated August 7, 2017 tiled "Beware of PI Con-Artists";*

g. *Posting dated August 21, 2017 titled "Freedom of Speech Under Attack";*

h. *Posting dated August 26, 2017 on the Facebook group "Canada Court Watch";*

i. *Posting dated September 4, 2017 titled "Intimidation Tactics by Dianna Holden";*

j. *Posting dated September 10, 2017 titled "Criminal Harassment (AKA Stalking) Laws in Canada"; and*

k. *Various posts on Facebook, Brainsyntax and elsewhere respecting Holden and NPL.*

You can read the full judgement on the website CanLii.org.

One would think that once you have been sued for Defamation, and you lose, that you would just stop conducting the behaviour to which got you in the mess in the first place. You would think this would be the end. Nope, it was not even close to being the end.

You see even after the trial, things started happening. Lee Hanlon, made three police reports alleging that I was harassing him. He further made three complaints to Consumer Protection British Columbia, and then of course he was also making complaints to my PI regulatory bodies. Even after I obtain a permanent Supreme Court Injunction prohibiting him from continuing on his escapade.

~ Eight ~

THE REGULATORY COMPLAINTS

THE REGULATORY COMPLAINTS

Immediately proceeding the judgement being rendered, I actually thought finally this chapter would be done. That Lee Hanlon, would have moved on and just got on with his life, as I certainly tried to. I was naive in thinking this because it was anything from the contrary. I ended up changing my name, my business name and started to rebuild my brand.

All of a sudden, in March of 2019, I received notification by Consumer Protection British Columbia, my regulatory body for my collection agency, that Lee Hanlon, had made three complaints to them. These complaints stemmed from me trying to collect the outstanding judgement and costs that had been awarded to me. A mysterious email was produced by Lee, which led me to hiring a Forensic Computer company to analyze my computer email, which resulted in their findings that someone had purportedly placed this email on my business email server to make it appear that the email had been written and sent by me when it had not been.

Then there were the complaints Lee, made to my Private Investigator Regulatory body, which again were deemed as unfounded. Lee, took it further and again launched multiple complaints with the RCMP (Royal Canadian Mounted Police) alleging that I was criminally harassing him and stalking him. None of these complaints went anywhere, as they were all deemed unfounded. That being stated it continued to give me stress and I began to think this just will never end. I couldn't figure out why he continued to harass me this way. Lee, even went to his local Member of Legislative Assembly to complain about me.

Lee, just never gives up. I again contacted the Burnaby RCMP, to try to have Lee, charged criminally, because what he was doing and continues to do just was not right. You would think that I would get justice in some capacity. Burnaby RCMP, also forwarded criminal charges to the Crown Prosecutor office, but they stated it wasn't in the public interest. Once again, he was not charged. I then tried to file a private information, meaning a private prosecution. I took everything to the courts with me to finally put a end to this saga, but once again Crown shut it down claiming not in the public interest.

Going through this really takes an emotional toll on you. You do everything right, and try to go through all the legal avenues you have available to you, and it just gets squashed every which way. No wonder why Lee, continues what he does. He had no consequences for his actions.

As a licensed private investigator, I thought that I could provide the judgement to my own regulatory body, which clearly states that he enlisted employees to steal documents from my business, as well that it clearly states that Lee Hanlon, acted with malice and made defamatory statements about me and my businesses.

It also showed that Lee Hanlon was not of good character based on his actions, but even my complaints to my regulatory body went ignored. They viewed it as due to him acting in a "Personal Capacity" and not that of a "Security Worker", engaged in security work, that they would decline to investigate. I respect my regulatory body, but I truly feel that our director erred in her decision. What does one do when the deck is stacked against you. You do everything you can in your power to make someone stop harassing you, and it all falls on deaf ears. Nothing!. There is nothing a victim can do to get justice when no one will take action. There is no justice, as the Prosecutors office in British Columbia, picks and chooses which cases they will approve charges on. They don't even allow private prosecutions in our country and continuously stay them.

No matter how I tried, the evidence I provided to my regulatory body they refused to remove his licensure. What was completely screwed with this process was that it was proven in Supreme Court that:
 a) He posted statements that were false
 b) He had contacted staff members of my business and got them to steal documents from my business that did not belong to him.
 c) That he acted with malice

d) He made false statements to police about me and the reports were deemed unfounded.

None of this mattered to my regulatory body, and they continued to license him knowing all of this. All because they believed he was acting in a personal capacity, yet every time he spoke of me he would flash his PI License and state he was investigating me yet he had no client. He was on a personal vendetta to harm my business and reputation.

Meanwhile, I was left with a 70 thousand dollar legal bill, had to charge my name, my business name etc. and Lee Hanlon, had no consequences. He can still sit behind a keyboard, and play keyboard warrior. He can still work as a licensed private investigator, and have no accountability for the havoc he wreaked on my life.

I have respect for my regulatory body, and for me being a private investigator is a privilege, that being stated I believe they should have investigated this entire matter adequately and swiftly. I feel that by the regulatory body not taking action it was condoning Lee's behaviour and continued behaviour, because there were no consequences for his actions. I do not feel that I had a fair administrative process with my complaints. My complaints were well founded with substantial evidence to back them up. The fact that he continuously utilized the fact he was a licensed private investigator to harass me, in my opinion made it a regulatory body issue.

As a private investigator we have a code of conduct. In the code of conduct it states that we cannot make false complaints to police, and be of good character. How could they deem that he was of good character given everything that he did to me and continues to do to me.

To add insult to injury in August of 2020, they licensed his security business Securus Research as a licensed private investigation agency. How is it that he can be trusted with working in a highly respected industry with the conduct that he exhibits.

During the 4 1/2 years of being licensed as a Private Investigator, I have never had a client complaint about my work or my business. However, my own regulatory body investigated my agency because I had an employee that they alleged was collecting Employment Insurance benefits and was not declaring their income. They gave me a warning ticket because I did not ask this employee if they were collecting Employment Insurance. I disputed this warning ticket because quite frankly it is not up to me declare an employees income to employment insurance. It is up to them to fully disclose all income they receive. I did my part as a business owner by documenting all hours worked by this employee and all monies paid to this employee. As well, I had an employee who had a fake security worker license. I checked the license number on my regulatory body website, which told me that the license was valid. Yet it turned out he had created a false license.

Again, how is that my fault when our own regulatory body does not depict pictures of the security workers. I was written a warning ticket on this as well. Again, I wrote a dispute to this because at the time it appeared to be the old license style to which was issued. As well, as this security worker worked for multitudes of companies and some of them had been around for years, and they too hired the same person. Again, I was the one that was reprimanded for this. No other company was. In my opinion this was not a fair administrative justice.

EMOTIONAL TOLL

~ Nine ~

EMOTIONAL TOLL

When you are the victim of defamation whether it be online or in print, it really plays with your emotions. It attacks your self-esteem, and you feel worthless. During the course of all the statements Lee, made online about me, as I watched people commenting on his posts in the various Facebook groups he was a part of. Where he was typing these words to anyone in the world that would read them it was really tough. Cyberbullying, is not a victimless crime.

Words hurt, even on a screen. It is so difficult to digest how mean people that you don't even know can be. I regularly would see people chime in on his posts that didn't even know me and comment about me in a derogatory way. It was so difficult for me to not post myself, but I chose to stay silent online as I didn't want to give Lee Hanlon, ammunition to say it was tit for tat.

The way Lee, mis-interpreted emails sent to him by me, which were outlined in the trial, was very disturbing. Lee, didn't think about my children who were reading this shit. He didn't think about how I would lay in bed at night wanting to commit suicide because of what he was saying. I could not understand why he targeted me. He was a licensed Private Investigator, he was supposed to be a professional. Clearly from his actions he was no professional.

His need for attention, his need to hurt me, I don't know where it came from. I like to see the good in people, At least I try to. I don't understand his reason behind what he has done, but he doesn't stop, and I doubt he ever will. What is scary is that I allowed him to effect me. I allowed the words to hurt me. He got under my skin.

One thing I have learned through this entire process is that you cannot change someone else. You cannot stop them from posting lies about you and you cannot stop them from writing what they do, but what you can do is choose on how you will react. This is what I did. I chose what I would do about it, how I would react to it, and I did not allow what he has done to destroy my inner core. I choose to survive this. As difficult it is I never stooped to his level. I never retaliated, I never acted unethically, and I certainly did not take things outside of the law.

The fact that I have never retaliated speaks volumes, as it keeps my character and dignity intact. For me that was important. If there is anything I can tell someone who has went through what I have been going through is that you cannot control what is said, or printed but you can choose to not respond. Don't post and don't engage with anyone who is cyberbullying you. Do not show them it affects you. As they don't care and it just makes it worse.

Know that you are not alone when you are being bullied online. Tell someone about it. For me I think I am thick skinned. Now I am not going to say it didn't affect me it did. His words affected my business, and me personally. I lost a lot of business because of his actions, but that is something that can be built back up. People who know me personally know that I am not this person that he has portrayed.

It truly is an emotional rollercoaster. Even long after the trial, its now 2020, and the trial was in 2018, and it still has a huge impact on my life. After Lee, filed personal bankruptcy, I ended up retaining another lawyer to oppose his bankruptcy discharge.

Even since the trial, I have had more issues. Despite the Supreme Court Injunction prohibiting Lee, from continuing the defamatory words, he just changed the platform he used. He now does it through word of mouth and private messages once he vets you to determine you are not me. I didn't get justice in this matter, but it may come one day. Whatever the way it may come it remains to be seen.

I try to tell myself that this will all end one day. That I will look back at it and laugh and think just what a crazy situation it was. I sometimes think that one day Lee, will get what he deserves as he may piss of the wrong person. That being said, that day has not come as of yet.

I am to hurt to be angry, I am to hurt to hold a grudge. I cannot fathom how anyone can treat someone the way he has me. I have to have empathy, because if I don't then it will hurt more than the words on the screen. I have to have empathy because normal people don't just become keyboard warriors and intentionally hurt people unless they have an underlying condition. It is not normal to do this. For now I just try to let the emotional impact of his actions not affect me. At times it is so difficult to do but I also feel that I am a better person by not stooping to the level he has. During the trial, Lee Hanlon, alleged he was getting threats from the Hells Angel's organization, I thought it was amusing given the fact I am not affiliated in any capacity with that organization. This shows what kind of paranoia Lee Hanlon, had over the situation.

I think that when someone is harassing you online, and you just are at your wits end its best to talk to someone about it, don't keep it inside because it eats at you. It can tear you a part emotionally. People don't understand words on a screen do hurt, they affect people. It is easy when you are typing to type whatever you have no emotional connection, however when reading someone's words about you that are malicious and untruthful it really cuts you to the bone.

Cyberbullying has led some people to commit suicide. It is important to think before you type on a keyboard and start cyberbullying someone. Your words can have nasty consequences on the other end.

~ Ten ~

THE AFTERMATH

Thinking that I had finally received a bit of justice when I obtained my court order judgement, I truly thought this would be the end of my dealings with Lee Hanlon. Unfortunately, it didn't end up that way. You see when you obtain a judgement you need to collect the money that is owed to you. In order to do that you need to ether garnishee an employment or banking. Unfortunately, for me I couldn't. You see Lee Hanlon, stated he had no money, and then he filed for personal bankruptcy. WHAM!!!! Slap in the face again.

What do you do when you are being harassed and stalked online by a Licensed Private Investigator, what do you do when you have taken every legal mechanism available to you within the confines of the law to protect yourself and your business, your family and your friends. Truly, there is nothing you can do. In my case the aftermath of it all was that Lee Hanlon, can continue doing everything he does, posting online, making false statements about me, talking to everyone and anyone who will listen to him and I cannot do nothing about it.

When you have a private investigator harassing you and stalking you online, there is really nothing you can do about it. Police recommended charges a second time against Lee Hanlon, those as well did not go anywhere. I filed a private prosecution again didn't go anywhere. I complained to my MLA, my MP, again it didn't go anywhere. The irony of it all, I am not the only one. Lee Hanlon, has posted stuff about others, in the same capacity he has of me. He has made complaint after complaint about my lawyers, he has made statements online about the presiding Judge and my lawyers, to which my lawyers went back and got a court order prohibiting him from continuing to post about them too.

I do believe justice will come his way. I am uncertain at what time, how or where, I have to believe in the judicial process and system. I choose to hold my head high, and not allow him to continue this tirade of harassment. I will continue to run my businesses, I will continue to help my clients. I will succeed regardless of what Lee Hanlon, continues to do towards me.

One day he will meet someone bigger and badder than me. One day he will say the wrong thing to someone else, and they will not go to the police, they will not sue him, then he will get justice in whatever way that looks like. Karma is a bitch. What comes around goes around. I don't have to do anything, because he will dig his own dirty little mess and I will feel good when that day comes. Mainly, knowing that I did not step outside the realms of the law, I did not take street justice, as so many people suggested. I did not steep to his level. That gives me satisfaction. After all, why would I want to give Lee Hanlon, the ammunition he wants.

One thing I have learned throughout the entire process of having to deal with this horrendous situation is this. Anyone can write on the internet about you things and you can let it get to you or you can do something about it. But one thing you cannot control in life, is whether or not the court of public opinion will believe what they read about you. I know people who personally know me know I am a standup ethical person. I would give my shirt on my back for someone in need. I am a workaholic, I work hours on end and don't even bill most of my time.

I became a private investigator to help people. I am not in it for the money. If one case helps someone for me that is all that matters. Over the last 4 1/2 years, I have developed strong business relationships, I have developed a ton of references. I am okay!!!.

Lee Hanlon, did not win....... I did.... There will always be Lee Hanlon's in this world, and there will always be someone out there that will take up a keyboard and type away. You need to learn on how to deal with it, and not let it get to you. You need to forgive and not forget. I forgive Lee, for every key stroke he has done. I forgive him for making my life hell. I thank him for making me stronger today then any other day. In all his posts and all the shit that he has done it has made me stronger. It enabled me to work even harder, because I had to overcome the damage he did. Lee Hanlon, was the driving force in me working my ass off to get to where I am today. I am a fighter, I am strong. I will however NEVER, forget what Lee Hanlon did.

~ Eleven ~

COURT JUDGEMENT

IN THE SUPREME COURT OF BRITISH COLUMBIA

Citation:	Holden v. Hanlon,
	2019 BCSC 622

Between:

Date: 20190423
Docket: S177372 Registry: Vancouver

Plaintiffs

Dianna Leigh Holden, also known as Jolene Johnson, NPL Services Inc., and 0845450 BC Ltd., operating as National People Locator

And

Defendants

Lee Hanlon, also known as Martello Leroi Franks, also known as Marty Franks, and Vincent Schiele

Before: The Honourable Madam Justice Dardi

Reasons for Judgment

Counsel for the Plaintiffs:	T. Brayer K. Wang
The Defendant, Lee Hanlon, appearing in person:	L. Hanlon
The Defendant, Vincent Schiele:	No appearance
Place and Date of Trial:	Vancouver, B.C. August 7-10 and 23, 2018
Written Submissions:	September 14, 2018
Place and Date of Judgment:	Vancouver, B.C. April 23, 2019

Table of Contents

INTRODUCTION..4
PROCEDURAL HISTORY.. 5
Private Investigator   Licensing.. 6
Licences..9
Interactions between Mr. Hanlon and Ms. Holden....................11
Evidence of Olivia Hanson..13
Electronic Documents..14
Other Evidentiary Matters... 16
ALLEGED DEFAMATORY POSTINGS................................17
Pleadings..17
Publication..17
ISSUES..37
LEGAL FRAMEWORK..39
Were the statements defamatory?....................................40
Did the statements refer to the plaintiffs?................................... 41
Publication.. 41
Defences.. 41
ANALYSIS..44

- Claim against Hanlon................................... 44

Position of the Parties... 44
The Allegedly Defamatory Statements................................ 44
Summary of Claim against Mr. Hanlon..........................61

- Claim by the Corporate Plaintiffs................................... 62

- Claim against Mr. Schiele.. 62

DAMAGES... 66
  Legal Framework.. 66
  General Damages... 66
  Aggravated Damages.. 69
  Punitive Damages... 71
  Assessed Jointly or Individually...................................... 71
  Position of the Parties... 73
    Ms. Holden... 73
    Mr. Hanlon... 73
  Assessment of Damages Against Mr. Hanlon................. 74
  Aggravated Damages.. 77
  Punitive Damages... 77

Assessment of Damages Against Mr. Schiele.................. 78
    INJUNCTION.. 79

INTRODUCTION

- These proceedings spring from a series of postings made by the defendant, Lee Hanlon, on various social media platforms and internet discussion forums. The postings were made in 2016 and 2017. The plaintiff, Dianna Holden, alleges that the series of unfounded and unsubstantiated allegations in the publications were defamatory and damaged her personal reputation and the reputation and viability of her

- Holden, who resides in Abbotsford, British Columbia, is the sole director of the two corporate plaintiffs, 0845450 BC Ltd. ("084"), a people locating and process serving agency, and NPL Services Inc. ("NPL"), which formerly offered private investigation ("PI") services. She currently operates a third company, National Risk Management Group Limited ("NRMG"), which is not a plaintiff in this action. It has assumed the private investigation aspects of Ms. Holden's business. After the she launched this litigation, Ms. Holden changed her name to Jolene Johnson. She continues to use Dianna Holden on her passport and bank accounts.

- The plaintiffs seek general, aggravated and punitive damages as well as a permanent injunction against Mr. Hanlon and Mr. Schiele. The plaintiffs' contempt application against Mr. Hanlon was adjourned generally by

- Hanlon, who describes himself as a security professional, appeared at trial in person. He resides in Mission, British Columbia. Mr. Hanlon does not dispute that he wrote and posted the statements that are the subject matter of this litigation. His overarching submission is that he is shielded from liability because the impugned statements are all true.

- The defendant, Vincent Schiele, resides in Ontario and is alleged to be the "owner and operator" of the website brainsyntax.com ("Brainsyntax"). Brainsyntax is one of the online forums on which some of the allegedly defamatory statements were posted. The website is akin to a forum where users may post articles and links, and has the tagline "a voice & advocate of the oppressed".

- Schiele, who is also self-represented, did not appear at trial. He filed a response to civil claim on September 8, 2017. He was personally served with the Notice of Trial and the plaintiffs' trial brief on May 31, 2018. He did not appear at the trial management conference on June 27, 2018. Mr. Schiele did not respond to the notice to admit, dated July 19, 2018, which was served on him, along with the second amended notice of civil claim on July 20, 2018, pursuant to Master Scarth's order.

- The action has been discontinued against the other named

PROCEDURAL HISTORY

- On October 5, 2017, Mr. Justice Sewell granted an interlocutory order in this proceeding, enjoining Mr. Hanlon from continuing to post statements relating to Ms. Holden on the internet. The order reads, inpart:
    1. Lee Hanlon or any agent of Hanlon's SHALL BE ENJOINED FROM either directly or indirectly, writing, publishing, posting or in any way distributing or making public any accusatory or disparaging allegations regarding the honesty, trustworthiness or alleged improper behaviour of Dianna Holden, NPL Services Inc. and National People Locator in any forum of any kind whatever and enjoining Hanlon from directing or assisting others in writing, publishing posting to the Internet or in any way distributing or making public such allegations until further order of the Court;

2. *Within 48 hours hours [sic] of the date of this order, Hanlon shall remove all publications he has made on the Internet on websites including but not limited to Craigslist.com, Facebook.com, LinkedIn.com, Brainsyntax.com and Securusresearch.wixsite.com/mysite respecting Holden, NPL and National PeopleLocator...*

- The plaintiffs discontinued their claims against Her Majesty the Queen in Right of British Columbia on April 5,

- Following a three-day summary trial application that was heard in February and March 2018, Mr. Justice Crossin, in oral reasons for judgment delivered on April 5, 2018, dismissed the plaintiffs' summary trial application. Although he filed a response and affidavit material, Mr. Schiele did not attend the

- Pursuant to a consent order pronounced on June 27, 2018, Master Scarth set aside the plaintiffs' default judgment and dismissed the claims against Lorelai Edwards.

- The claims against Patricia Pelley, Facebook Inc., and Google Inc. were discontinued on July 19,

OVERVIEW

- In these Reasons, the summary of facts reflects evidence that was either not in dispute, or, where it was in dispute, the factual findings I have made based on the consideration of the evidence as a whole. I have explained the reasoning underlying my findings where the evidence conflicted in a significant way on material points, or a party has urged that a particular inference be drawn from the

- For the most part the plaintiffs rely on the deemed falsity of the allegedly defamatory statements. The plaintiffs adduced scant documentary evidence to counter Mr. Hanlon's contention that the impugned statements were

- Some of Ms. Holden's conduct in response to Mr. Hanlon's allegedly defamatory publications, such as her messages to Mr. Hanlon as Tamara Samuels, was misguided. Although it is a consideration to be weighed in the Court's overall assessment, I have concluded that any shortcomings and inconsistencies in Ms. Holden's evidence were not particularly significant in the context of the evidence as a

- Overall Ms. Holden left the Court with the impression that she was genuinely attempting to answer questions truthfully and accurately. Generally, I found her evidence on material points to be

Private Investigator Licensing

- Private investigators are required to be licensed in B.C. Their licensing is governed by the Security Services Act, S.B.C. 2007, c. 30 [SSA], and is administered by the Security Programs Division of the Ministry of Justice. There are

two categories of licences: under supervision, and fully licensed. The under supervision employees must be supervised by a fully licenced private investigator.

- Section 1 of the SSA defines "security work" as follows:

"security work" means the work of, or any aspect of the services provided by, any of the following:

- an armoured car guard service;
- a locksmith;
- a private investigator;
- a security alarm service;
- a security consultant;

- a security guard service;
- a body armour salesperson;

- The requirement to obtain a security worker's licence is under s. 2 of the SSA:

Security worker licence required
2 An individual must not engage in any kind of security work, or hold himself or herself out to be so employed or employable, unless

- the individual holds a valid security worker licence for that kind of security work,
- the individual is exempt by regulation from the requirement to hold a security worker licence, or
- the registrar determines that the security work in which the individual is engaged is incidental to the individual's primary

- The requirements for obtention of a security worker's licence are contained within the Security Services Regulation, B.C. Reg. 207/2008 (the "Regulation"). The two licence categories that are relevant to this action are "private investigator" and "private investigator under supervision".

4	Private investigator	Doing the work of, and providing any aspect of the services provided by, a private investigator
5	Private investigator under supervision	Doing the work of, and providing any aspect of the services provided by, a private investigator, but only while under the supervision of an individual who holds a security worker licence described in item 4 of this table

- The requirements for a "private investigator's licence" are as follows:

Qualifications for a licence 3. ...

- An applicant is qualified for a security worker licence of the type described in item 4 of the table if the applicant
  - has sufficient fluency in the English language to be able to converse in English with the public while carrying out his or her duties, and
  - either
    - has both
      - two years experience or more working as or providing the services of a private investigator, and
      - successfully completed courses in evidence gathering and presentation and in the aspects of criminal and civil law that are relevant to the work of a private investigator, or
    - demonstrates to the satisfaction of the registrar that he or she has experience equivalent to the experience and training referred to in subparagraph (i).

- The Security Services branch of the Ministry of Justice has published licensing policies (the "Policies") regarding qualifications for a private investigator's licence. The Policies read, in part:

- In order to be qualified for a private investigator security worker licence, an applicant must meet one of the following training and/or experience requirements:
  - two years of documented experience providing the services of a private investigator or private investigator under supervision, ending not more than five years prior to the date of the application, and successful completion of recognized courses in evidence gathering and presentation and in the aspects of criminal and civil law that are relevant to the work of a private investigator in B.C. or Security Licensing Process and Licence Conditions Policies Section 2
  - ten years of experience performing general police duties in a Canadian police force and proof of registration in the Private Security Training Network on-line course, "Introduction to Private Investigation", (course/exam must be completed within the first year of licensing) or
  - knowledge and experience equivalent to that which would be obtained under paragraph (a)

[Emphasis added.]

- In order to obtain a private investigator licence in British Columbia, an individual must meet the conditions and requirements under SSA such as providing authorizations for the registrar to carry out criminal record checks. They are also required to outline their previous work experience. The individual must complete an online course, followed by an exam proctored at the Justice Institute. This allows an individual to obtain a private investigator under supervision licence. In order to obtain a full unsupervised private investigator licence, an individual typically must complete two years of supervision under a licenced private investigator. Alternatively, if an individual demonstrates to the licencing body that they have sufficient knowledge, skills and experience, this requirement may be

- Pursuant to s. 4(1) of the SSA, the registrar may refuse to issue or renew a security worker licence. The relevant provisions provide as follows:

Refusal of security worker licences

4 (1) The registrar may refuse to issue or renew a security worker licence if any of the following apply:

- the applicant or licensee fails in any way to comply with or does not meet the requirements of section 3 [applying for security worker licence];
- the registrar considers that the applicant's or licensee's conduct, education training, experience, skill, mental condi-

tion, character or repute makes it undesirable that he or she be licensed;
- the registrar considers that it is not in the public interest that the applicant or licensee be licensed;
- the registrar is satisfied that the licensee has done something that
  - justifies refusal to renew a licence to the licensee,
  - contravenes a provision of this Act or the regulations, or
  - contravenes a condition of the licence;
- the applicant or licensee is charged with or convicted of a crime;
- the applicant is a peace
- The registrar may hold a hearing before making a decision under subsection (1).
- The registrar must give the applicant or licensee written reasons for a decision under subsection (1).

Licences

- Holden applied for her PI licence on March 11, 2016. Ms. Holden had previous work experience in the following areas:
- private investigation agency, named Brian Brown & Associates from approximately 1994 to 1996. She also worked for Cromwell Security and Investigations. The evidence does not establish the time frame that she worked for this
- she was a loss prevention officer for Overwaitea Food Group and Army and Navy, from 1996 to

- she was a licenced debt collector employed by a debt collections agency in 1996. She was licenced for this service under the Business Practices and Consumer Protection Act, S.B.C. 2004, c.
- she privately offered skip-tracing services and was hired by legal professionals to locate individuals for serving legal documents or debt collection, for approximately twenty years, beginning in the early

- On May 30, 2016, Ms. Holden received her full private investigator's licence without having to meet the requirements set out in Policy 2.6.2.1(a) or (b). She satisfied the registrar that she had the equivalent knowledge and experience, under Policy 2.6.2.1(c). She was not required to complete the usual supervision period prior to obtaining a full

- The plaintiff, 084, was incorporated on February 21, 2009, and operated as a skip-tracing agency under the name National People Locator. This company, as a skip-tracing agency, essentially provided a service for locating individuals on behalf of private

- In July 2016, following Ms. Holden's obtention of a private investigator's licence, NPL was incorporated. On July 6, 2016, NPL was licenced as a private investigation and security company. This a separate licencing requirement under the governing legislation. In May 2018, the private investigation branch of the company, along with its licence, was transferred to NRMG, a newly incorporated entity. As I mentioned earlier, NRMG is not a plaintiff. NPL was reconfigured to providing debt collection and bailiff services. Ms. Holden is the sole shareholder of both 084 and NRMG.

- From July 2016 until early 2018, NPL employed between two and six employees at various times, not including Ms. Holden, who also provided services to the company. This included three private investigators; one of whom was fully licenced under the SSA and two of whom were licenced as private investigators under

Interactions between Mr. Hanlon and Ms. Holden

- Hanlon, a veteran with the Canadian Forces Reserve, has been licenced as a fully licenced private investigator since November 2014. He received his under supervision licence in September 2012. He is a basic security training instructor and has an advanced security training certification. He also worked for sixteen years as a security guard. He obtained a bachelor of general studies with a major in criminology from the University of the Fraser Valley. He worked as a paralegal for eight years. He took one year of law school, through an external online program offered through the University of London. Since June 2017, he has been employed at a security firm in the Fraser Valley.

- On September 19, 2011, Mr. Hanlon contacted Ms. Holden online via a Facebook message. They interacted for approximately four days. Mr. Hanlon commenced the conversation, and they corresponded regarding, among other things, his work as an "advocate".

- Holden did not have contact with Mr. Hanlon again until February 21, 2016, when Ms. Holden responded to Mr. Hanlon's Craigslist posting requesting information pertaining to the Highway of Tears investigation. According to

Ms. Holden, for safety reasons, she responded using a false name and a false email account. Once the parties realized that they had previously interacted, their discussion turned to other topics. They eventually met at Ms. Holden's apartment sometime in March or April 2016, and they had a discussion regarding, among other things, business opportunities and the possibility of working together. This was their only in-person meeting.

- *In mid-March 2016, Mr. Hanlon encouraged Ms. Holden to apply for a private investigator licence. On April 3, 2016, they had discussions regarding Ms. Holden*

employing Mr. Hanlon as a loss prevention officer. However, nothing materialized at that time.

- *On April 14, 2016, Ms. Holden sent her application to the Security Programs Division, the licencing body for private investigators. In her application, she explained how her previous work experience would be equivalent to the 2000-hour requirement for a full private investigator licence. On May 7, 2016, and in response to the various scenarios posed, Ms. Holden submitted further documentation to the Security Programs Division. Ms. Holden maintains that all the statements in her application are*

- *A former employee of Ms. Holden's appears to have sent a copy of*

Ms. Holden's application documents to Mr. Hanlon through a Facebook message. This was done without Ms. Holden's authorization. Mr. Hanlon does not dispute that he received a copy of these documents.

- On April 23, 2016, Mr. Hanlon sent an email to Ms. Holden demanding that she cease any further communications with

- The parties did not have any further contact until early June 2016, when Mr. Hanlon reached out to Ms. Holden to "try this again, with a clean slate".

Ms. Holden refused to send Mr. Hanlon a copy of her private investigator licence until he agreed to her terms of employment. On June 8, 2016, Mr. Hanlon told her he was not interested in such an opportunity. Ms. Holden responded on the same date with a cease and desist letter, requesting that Mr. Hanlon refrain from any form of communication with either herself or her businesses.

- The allegedly defamatory postings commenced in late July 2016. Substantially all of the alleged incidents involve online postings, either on social media platforms, online discussion forums or the personal website of the The alleged defamation took place over the course of approximately 14 months, from July 2016 until September 2017.

- Holden made a complaint against Mr. Hanlon with the Abbotsford Police Department. Mr. Hanlon was investigated by the Abbotsford Police Department for defamatory libel, under s. 298 of the Criminal Code, R.S.C. 1985, c. C-46 [Criminal Code]. The Abbotsford Police Department recommended that charges be laid.

However, the Crown ultimately decided not to approve the Abbotsford Police Department's charge recommendation.

Evidence of Olivia Hanson

- Olivia Hanson, a former employee of NPL, worked for NPL from August 2017 until May 2018. Originally, she worked in sales and marketing, and then later transitioned into an administrative role. Ms. Hanson described NPL as a "toxic company".

- According to Ms. Hanson, Ms. Holden would often join in on sales calls, and would inform the client that she had been wrongfully defamed. Ms. Holden denied having had any such discussion with clients in Ms. Hanson's presence. She maintained that the only time she would discuss the alleged defamatorystatements is on those occasions that a client, having viewed some of Mr. Hanlon's articles online, would specifically raise the issue with

- *Hanson also alleged that Ms. Holden created false accounts on a credit score website named "Credit Karma", in order to obtain credit scores of an individual. Ms. Holden denies having done this, and stated that the only credit score searches she has undertaken were properly done through Equifax andTransUnion.*

- *On cross-examination, Ms. Hanson admitted that she took documents and emails from her former employer, as she believed it was her duty under the Employment Standards Act, R.S.B.C. 1996, c. 113, to report a crime. She believed that "[Ms. Holden] was committing a crime" because she "witnessed her trying to frame [Mr. Hanlon] by setting up a fake email account under his name and trying to claim that he was practicing law".*

- *Hanson presented as a disgruntled former employee. Her clear lack of objectivity coupled with the lack of any objective evidence to support her assertions significantly compromised her credibility. Overall, I found her assertions did not accord with the preponderance of probabilities associated with the case as a whole.*

- *Where her evidence conflicts with that of Ms. Holden, hers must be rejected as not being*

Electronic Documents

- Much of the evidence submitted by both parties consisted of electronic documents in the form of screenshots. These screenshots documented both the allegedly defamatory postings and the communications between the parties on the Facebook Messenger app. The authenticity or integrity of this evidence was not challenged by either party. In any case, I have concluded that the electronic documentary evidence adduced at trial, except where otherwise noted, is properly admissible, as it conforms to the requirements of the Canada Evidence Act, R.S.C. 1985, c. C-5 [CEA].

- The CEA requires an electronic document to be authentic and to meet the common law "best evidence" rule. The pertinent provisions state as follows:

Authentication of electronic documents

- Any person seeking to admit an electronic document as evidence has the burden of proving its authenticity by evidence capable of supporting a finding that the electronic document is that which it is purported to

Application of best evidence rule — electronic documents

31.2(1) The best evidence rule in respect of an electronic document is satisfied

- on proof of the integrity of the electronic documents system by or in which the electronic document was recorded or stored; ...

Printouts

(2) Despite subsection (1), in the absence of evidence to the contrary, an electronic document in the form of a printout satisfies the best evidence rule if the printout has been manifestly or consistently acted on, relied on or used as a record of the information recorded or stored in the printout.

Presumption of integrity

- For the purposes of subsection 31.2(1), in the absence of evidence to the contrary, the integrity of an electronic documents system by or in which an electronic document is recorded or stored is proven
    - by evidence capable of supporting a finding that at all material times the computer system or other similar device used by the electronic documents system was operating properly or, if it was not, the fact of its not operating properly did not affect the integrity of the electronic document and there are no other reasonable grounds to doubt the integrity of the electronic documents system;

- *if it is established that the electronic document was recorded or stored by a party who is adverse in interest to the party seeking to introduce it; or*
- *if it is established that the electronic document was recorded or stored in the usual and ordinary course of business by a person who is not a party and who did not record or store it under the control of the party seeking to introduce*

- The threshold required by s. 31.1 has been described as "a low threshold";

the party seeking to admit the electronic document "does not need to prove that the electronic document is an exact and complete copy": R. v. Hamdan, 2017 BCSC 676 at para. 44.

- In v. Hirsch, 2017 SKCA 14, the Saskatchewan Court of Appeal described the low threshold for authentication in the following terms:

[18] ... Quite simply, to authenticate an electronic document, counsel could present it to a witness for identification and, presumably, the witness would articulate some basis for authenticating it as what it purported to be
(see: Pfizer Canada Inc. v Teva Canada Limited, 2016 FCA 161 at para 93. That is, while authentication is required, it is not an onerous requirement. In Watt's Manual, the author notes at 1115:
The burden of proving authenticity of an electronic document is on the person who seeks its admission. The standard of

proof required is the introduction of evidence capable of supporting a finding that the electronic document is as it claims to be. In essence, the threshold is met and admissibility achieved by the introduction of some evidence of authenticity.
[Emphasis in original.]

- All things considered I am satisfied that the authenticity of the printouts of the screenshots has been established in this case. Both Ms. Holden and Mr. Hanlon testified about the screenshots and referred to and relied on them without question throughout the proceedings. Moreover, with regards to the integrity of the documents, Mr. Hanlon, during his testimony, admitted to authoring and posting the alleged defamatory articles on various social media platforms that were introduced into evidence by Ms.

- In sum, I find that, except as otherwise noted in these Reasons, the authenticity of printed screenshots of the electronic documents has been established.

Other Evidentiary Matters

- Hanlon represented himself at trial. While some accommodation for self-represented persons may be appropriate, fairness of the trial process is the overarching consideration: Berezowski v. British Columbia (Residential Tenancy Branch), 2014 BCSC 363 at para. 178.

- At the outset of the trial I provided Mr. Hanlon with a written memorandum that summarized what the trial procedure would be, some important rules of evidence, and what his obligations

- Hanlon's evidence at trial included a significant amount of hearsay evidence. Despite repeated directions from the Court that hearsay evidence relied on for the truth of its contents is presumptively inadmissible, Mr. Hanlon, from time to time, attempted to rely on hearsay evidence to establish his defence of justification. The principal concern arising from the hearsay nature of the evidence is the inability of the other party to test the allegations of the declarant by way of cross-examination. In this case, as a matter of fairness to the plaintiffs, I am unable to take into account the hearsay evidence.

- Similarly, I raised the confrontation principle, commonly known as the rule in Browne v. Dunn, (1893) 6 R. 67 (H.L.), with Mr. Hanlon. I pointed out to him that if he intended to challenge Ms. Holden's credibility by calling contradictory evidence, as a matter of fairness she should be given the chance to address that contradictory evidence in cross-examination.

- Hanlon sought to introduce into evidence emails from Ms. Holden to Shaw Communications, the Law Society of B.C., and others, in which, among other things, Ms. Holden made allegations of wrongdoing by Mr. Hanlon. Mr. Hanlon is neither the recipient nor the author of these documents and the documents were not put to Ms. Holden in cross-examination. There is no principled basis upon which these documents were admissible at trial. In any event, and in light of the issues that I must decide in this case, these documents have no probative value.

- Finally, I note that I ruled that many of the documents adduced at trial were admissible only for establishing that the alleged defamatory statements were published. Importantly, the truth of the contents of the documents was not established by that admission into

ALLEGED DEFAMATORY POSTINGS

Pleadings

- In *Weaver v. Corcoran*, 2017 BCCA 160 [*Weaver*], Madam Justice Dickson expounded the critical importance of pleadings in defamation actions:
  - In defamation actions, pleadings are exceptionally important. This is due in part to the serious nature of defamation allegations and the significance of context in assessing them in an appropriately informed, well-balanced way. Traditionally, defamation pleadings have attracted a more critical evaluation than those in other causes and have been held to a higher standard regarding the precision with which material facts must be pleaded. This enhanced judicial scrutiny is justified based on the need to avoid unwarranted "fishing expeditions" and the critical importance of the defendant knowing clearly the case to be met: *Laufer v. Bucklaschuk* (1999), 181 D.L.R. (4th) 83 at para. 24 (M.B.C.A.); *The Catalyst Capital Group Inc. v. Veritas Investment Research Corporation*, 2017 ONCA 85 at paras. 22–25.
  - More recently, courts have applied greater flexibility when analysing defamation pleadings, at least in the early stages of a proceeding. While the need for enhanced scrutiny and precise pleadings remains, it is recognised that plaintiffs may be unable to provide full particulars of allegations prior to discovery. For this reason, where a plaintiff pleads a prima facie case of defamation, including all reasonably available particulars of defamatory material, the pleadings may stand despite a lack of detailed facts outside the plaintiff's knowledge: *Catalyst Capital Group* at paras. 25–29. Nevertheless, given the fundamental values at stake in a defamation action, it remains particularly important for parties to plead and adhere to clearly defined issues of fact and law.

Publication

- Publication does not occur until "the defamatory matter is brought by the defendant or his agent to the knowledge and understanding of some person other than the plaintiff: McNichol v. Grandy, [1931] S.C.R. 696 at 704 [McNichol].

- Publication of a hyperlink does not by itself constitute publication of a defamatory statement. In Malak v. Hanna, 2019 BCCA 106 [Malak], the Court of Appeal provides an instructive distillation of the governing principles:

[85] The question of whether a person who hyperlinks has "published" the material that can be accessed by clicking on the hyperlink was dealt with by the Supreme Court of Canada in Crookes v. Newton, 2011 SCC 47, [2011] 3 S.C.R. 269. The majority reasons of Justice Abella in that case support the following propositions:

- the use of a hyperlink to defamatory content does not, by itself, amount to publication even if the hyperlink is followed and the content accessed: paras. 14, 44;
- when a person follows a hyperlink to defamatory content it is the actual creator or poster of that content who has published the libel: para. 30;

- "Only when a hyperlinker presents content from the hyperlinked material in a way that actually repeats the defamatory content, should that content be considered to be 'published' by the hyperlinker": para. 42.

- Publication of a hyperlink on various social media platforms may support an inference that the readership of an original article was more widespread than in the absence of the hyperlink and thus, may be relevant to an assessment of damages. However, it cannot constitute publication for the purposes of establishing a claim in defamation.
- Publication requires that a plaintiff establish that an individual other than the plaintiff, viewed and understood the defamatory information. As was stated by Deschamps J. in Crookes v. Newton, 2011 SCC 47 [Newton]:
- Publication is not complete until someone other than the person referred to receives and understands the defamatory information. Thus, "to shout aloud defamatory words on a desert moor where no one hears them, is not a publication" (Gambrill v. Schooley, 93 Md. 48 (U.S. Md. C.A. 1901), at p. 60). In the context of the Internet, a simple reference, absent evidence that someone actually viewed and understood the defamatory information to which it directs third parties, is not publication of that

- In order to ground an action in British Columbia for the tort of defamation, a plaintiff must establish that the alleged defamatory postings on the internet were accessed and read by someone in British Columbia. In Crookes v. Yahoo, 2007 BCSC 1325, aff'd 2008 BCCA 165, [Crookes] the Court stated:

- With respect to internet communications, the site of the alleged defamation is where the damage to reputation occurs: Dow Jones Co. Inc. v. Gutnick, (2002), 194 Aust. L.R. 433 (H.C.); Barrick Gold Corp. v. Blanchard and Co., [2003] O.J. No. 5817 (S.C.). It is when a person downloads the

impugned material from the internet that the damage to the reputation maybe done, and it is at that time and place that the tort of defamation is committed.

- In Burke, Mr. Justice Burnyeat held that defamatory statements published on an internet site, on a server located outside British Columbia, but accessed and read by someone in British Columbia, will constitute a proceeding founded on a tort in British

- The realities of communication and dissemination of information on the internet cannot be ignored: Bernstein v. Poon, 2015 ONSC 155 at para. 94 [Bernstein]. Although there may be no direct evidence of how many individuals have viewed an individual post on a specific social media platform, this is not a bar to drawing an inference that the postings were in fact viewed. In Hee Creations Group Ltd. v. Chow, 2018 BCSC 260 [Chow], Mr. Justice Weatherill stated:

[78] While the court cannot presume that the Publications were read in British Columbia, it is open to the court to draw an inference from the other available evidence that they were.

- Justice Weatherill then referred to Newton, in which Deschamps J. stated the following at para.109:

Absent a presumption of publication, the requirements of the second component of publication can be satisfied either by adducing direct evidence or, and this more likely, by asking the court to draw an inference. Inferring that defamatory information has been read and understood is not new. In Gaskin, the Court, quoting Gatley on Libel and Slander, observed (at p. 300):

It is not necessary for the plaintiff in every case to prove directly that the words complained of were brought to the actual knowledge of some third person. If he proves facts from which it can reasonably be inferred that the words were brought to the knowledge of some third person, he will establish a prima facie case.

- In Chow, Mr. Justice Weatherill drew the following inference:

[85] Although there is no direct evidence that the Publications were read in British Columbia, I am satisfied from Emily's evidence on cross-examination that VanPeople.com is an online forum targeting Chinese people living in Vancouver and that I can reasonably draw the inference that the Publications, at least to the extent that they were posted on VanPeople, were

read by one or more persons in British Columbia. To find otherwise would be to ignore the realities of 21st century communications and internet -based publication: Bernstein, at para. 94.

- In the section that follows I will set out in chronological order the postings referred to in the third amended notice of civil claim. Mr. Hanlon does not dispute that he posted the various articles on the

- Before turning to the analysis, I will set out my findings of whether these various postings were published as that term is defined in the

- In the Analysis section of these Reasons, I will then address whether the impugned statements that are the subject of the claim are defamatory and the defence of justification. I will reference the various postings by the alphabetical letter assigned to them

a) E-mail to another private investigator

- On July 23, 2016, Mr. Hanlon sent an email to Mark Gruschynski, one of

Ms. Holden's longstanding business partners, and private investigator in Edmonton, Alberta. Ms. Holden has done skip tracing work for over 20 years for
Mr. Gruschynski. I reproduce the email here:

There's a PI named Dianna Holden (also runs National People Locators), who is committing fraud. her PI business is known as NPL Services, Inc (http://www.nplservicesinc.com/)

Ms. Holden apparently lied on her PI application and as soon as she was granted PI status she had NPL Services, Inc licensed to do PI services. You might want to compare the information on her website to the information on your website.

Ms. Holden has no formal PI training (she isn't even successful in locates/skip tracing), and she has no training in the PI services she claims to provide. Ms. Holden suffers from Agoraphobia, and Borderline Personality Disorder, and also exhibits Sociopathic characteristic traits (such as pathological lying and retaliating by making false police reports).

Further, according to BC Court searches (CSO) she had a total of 15 appearances in Criminal Court related to an 810 application, and has been in Civil Court at least 34 times related to small claims and bankruptcy matters where she was the Respondent and Judgements [sic] where [sic] ruled in favor of the Claimant in each matter.

She commits fraud against CRA as well as scams her clients by not refunding in relation to locate/skip trace assignments she fails to complete.

- Hanlon admits to having sent this email, and to being the author of the email. Ms. Holden received a copy of this email from Mr. Gruschynski.

- It was after obtaining this email that Ms. Holden made a complaint against Mr. Hanlon with the Abbotsford Police

Extent of the publication

- This email was sent to Mr. Gruschynski and was read by him. However, there is no evidence before the Court that, other than in relation to Ms. Holden's pursuit of legal action, it was read by a third party in British

- Applying the Crookes reasoning, I conclude that the alleged defamatory statements in the email cannot be the subject of a defamation claim in British Columbia.

b)   Craigslist posting

- On July 9, 2016, Mr. Hanlon posted a Craigslist advertisement entitled "SCAM ALERT: NPL SERVICES INC.". The posting appears to have been reposted on July 25, 2016. The posting read:

Beware Dianna Holden is a fraud and liar. She recently fraudulently obtained a Private Investigator Licence and established a Private Investigations Business.

She is not trained nor does she have the experience to successfully complete the investigations she's listed on her website. As well, she is the only individual that holds a BC Private Investigator Licence in her newly formed PI business. None of her staff are licensed to conduct private investigation services. She also claims to guarantee a refund to clients if she is not successful in her locates/skip trace files. However, she does not.

There are a number of victims that she owes several thousand dollars to, but these victims are afraid to take action due to the mental health condition Dianna Holden has. She fears leaving her place of residence, so there is no way she'll be able to conduct investigation services for any alleged clients.

Dianna Holden is also known to use her operational business budget to pay for her residential services (she has a commercial office separate and apart from her place of residence).

As well, for a newly licensed PI with little or no experience, she charges over

$90 per hour with a "subject to change without notice" on all her fees. Is this the type of PI you want to retain? If anyone has a problem with Dianna Holden and NLP Services, Inc, they should file a formal complaint with the BC Ministry of Justice Security Programs Division.

The below is the link to her investigation business website (everything on her website was copied from other website)

http://www.nplservicesinc.com/

- The title of this posting was later changed to "NPL SERVICES INC." and the content of the post was altered. Mr. Hanlon admits that he authored the original posting and that he subsequently edited the

Extent of the publication

- Although Mr. Hanlon never received any response to this posting through the Craigslist website, Mr. Hanlon did not dispute that others had seen this

- According to Ms. Holden, Craigslist Fraser Valley is viewed by individuals in the Lower

- Holden provided an undated screenshot of a Google search of "NPL Services Inc Dianna Holden", which discloses that the first search result is this Craigslist posting. As a result of Google searches and the Craigslist posting,

Ms. Holden was contacted by various people with questions regarding her integrity.

- Holden also provided a Craigslist search of "npl services", which discloses that the first result was the subject Craigslist posting together with NPL's advertisements.

- Although there is no evidence on the actual number of people who have read the posting, based upon the totality of the evidence I conclude that this posting was published. It can reasonably be inferred that this posting was read by one or more individuals in British

c)   Facebook Group Posts: United Victims of Dianna (Davidson Holden)

- From July 27, 2016, until at least August 9, 2016, a Facebook profile named "Lee Hanlon" posted various statements on a Facebook group named "United Victims of Dianna (Davidson Holden)". The posts include the following allegedly defamatory statements:

1. NPL's Investigation Agreement is "not an agreement that any credible PI would draft";

1. Hanlon made a complaint to the Security Programs Division Complaints Department;
2. Holden was given a licence despite the fact that she does not have education, training or experience;
3. Holden has mental health problems;
4. Holden has to be "dealt with" and gives "my profession" a bad name;
5. Holden made death threats in 2011;
6. Holden made false accusations about Mr. Hanlon;
7. Holden accused Mr. Hanlon of being a "killer targeting witnesses on Craigslist";and
8. Holden must be "stopped".

- Hanlon admits that he was the author of these posts.

Extent of the publication

- I accept Ms. Holden's evidence that various individuals contacted her to inquire about these Facebook

- The group was originally a "public" Facebook group, meaning that anyone with a Facebook profile could access the postings. However, at an unknown date, it was changed to a "closed" Facebook group, meaning that people who were not members of the group could not see the contents of the postings, nor the names of the members of the group. Many, though not all, of the posts list the number of "views" it obtained. One post, dated July 27, 2016, was seen 6 times and had 3 comments; two others, dated July 25, 2016, and July 29, 2016, were seen 7 times and had 10 comments,

- I am satisfied on the totality of the evidence that these Facebook posts were published and read by at least one individual in British

d) Article on brainsyntax.com: Dianne Holden has been targeting me since late 2011 when I was a Law Student

- On October 25, 2016, an article attributed to Lee Hanlon was posted on brainsyntax.com, the website owned by the defendant, Mr. Schiele. The article took issue with s. 300 of the Criminal Code, and alleged that Ms. Holden had filed a criminal libel complaint "in retaliation" to his actions. The article contained the following allegedly defamatory statements:

1. Entitled "Dianne Holden has been targeting me since late 2011 when I was a LawStudent";
2. Hanlon filed a complaint about Ms. Holden and her company;
3. Holden has "severe mental health disorders";
4. Holden "has been targeting [Mr. Hanlon] since late 2011";
5. Holden "created a fake [F]acebook account...as a Penticton lawyer...and started harassing" Mr. Hanlon;
6. The Law Society "made her delete the account" after Mr. Hanlon complained to it;
7. In 2011, Ms. Holden accused Mr. Hanlon of being an investigator for the Ministry of Children and Family Development;
8. Holden accused Mr. Hanlon of being "a rapist facing rape charges";
9. In 2016, Ms. Holden accused Mr. Hanlon "of being a killer targeting witnesses on[C]raigslist";
10. Holden "threatened [Mr. Hanlon's] life...under a fake [F]acebook account"; and
11. Holden accused Mr. Hanlon of being "as unstable as she is".

- This article was also posted with some alterations to LinkedIn, a professional networking website, under the title "Unfounded Allegations". Mr. Hanlon admits to posting the article on both brainsyntax.com and LinkedIn with the alterations set out at para. 92

Extent of the publication

- Based upon the totality of the evidence, I conclude that this posting was published. I can reasonably infer that this posting was read by one or more individuals in British

- The plaintiffs sought to enter a document purporting to state the number of visitors and subscribers on the brainsyntax.com website. I ruled that neither the authenticity nor the truth of the contents of the document was

- Accordingly, I find that there is no properly admissible evidence before the Court as to how many people viewed this article, although, as stated above, I can reasonably infer that it was, in fact,

e) *LinkedIn Article: Unfounded Allegations*

- On October 26, 2016, Mr. Hanlon posted an article on LinkedIn, an online professional networking website entitled "Unfounded Allegations". It was similar to the article posted on brainsyntax.com, and appears to be an abbreviated version. I reproduce the article in its entirety below:

Recently I filed a complaint regarding an Abbotsford private investigator named Dianna Holden of National People Locators and NPL Services, Inc. In retaliation Dianna Holden filed a criminal libel complaint (section 300 criminal code) against me. APD fell for it and actually recommended to Crown that I be charged under section 300 of the criminal code. Currently Crown is reviewing the file and it was suggested that Crown will make their decision by the end of October or the first week of November 2016.

Dianna Holden has severe mental health disorders and has been targeting me since late 2011 when I was a Law Student.

Originally I was going to keep silent on this, however, not long after she filed the criminal libel complaint she created a fake facebook account as Tamra Samuels working as a Penticton lawyer and started harassing me.

I notified the Law Society and they made her delete the account. the Police refused to take my complaint, giving me the excuse that it would be hard to prove in court.

As she's a licensed private investigator, she also comes under the jurisdiction of the Security Programs Division of the BC Ministry of Justice and Attorney General (BCJAG), they'll be more harsh on her than the LSBC.

Canada is supposed to be a free and democratical [sic] nation, unfortunately keeping s. 300 ccc on the books makes Canada more like China, USSR, or any one of the Islamic nations. At least NL Supreme Court got it right when they struck down s.301 ccc

- Hanlon admits that he is the author of the article and that it was posted to LinkedIn, Facebook and Twitter.

Extent of the publication

- There is no evidence before the Court as to the number of views this posting may have obtained, either on LinkedIn or on other social media

- Based upon the totality of the evidence, I conclude that this posting was published. It can reasonably be inferred that this posting was read by one or more individuals in British

- I note that the fact that Mr. Hanlon posted links to this article on his Facebook and Twitter accounts does not amount to "publication" of the defamatory words themselves: Newton at paras. 14,

f)   *Personal Website Article: Charter of Rights Freedom of Speech under Attack*

- On October 29, 2016, Mr. Hanlon posted an article to his personal website, ("securusresearch.wixsite.com/mysite"), called "Charter of Rights Freedom of Speech under Attack". This post was updated on December 13, 2016. This post was also posted to LinkedIn, under the title "Gender Bias in Canada's Justice System". Therein, he wrote the following allegedly defamatory statements:

1. Holden has severe mental health disorders;
2. Holden is delusional;
3. Holden is targeting and harassing Mr. Hanlon;
4. In 2011, Ms. Holden accused Mr. Hanlon of being an investigator for MCFD;
5. In 2011, Ms. Holden accused Mr. Hanlon of targeting members of a Facebook page made for people with disputes with MCFD to find support;
6. Holden created a fake Facebook account to sexually harass Mr. Hanlon;
7. Holden accused Mr. Hanlon of targeting young girls via the internet in 2011;
8. Holden accused Mr. Hanlon of being the target of an investigation by the Law Society of BC in 2011;
9. Holden threatened Mr. Hanlon's life in 2011;
10. Law Enforcement will not investigate Mr. Hanlon's allegations because Ms. Holden used fake accounts;

11. Holden accused Mr. Hanlon of being a killer targeting witnesses in 2016;
12. In 2016, Ms. Holden made false accusations and harassed Hanlon and made a fake Facebook account for this purpose;

1. The Law Society of BC accepted a complaint made by Mr. Hanlon about Ms. Holden and made the Ms. Holden delete a fake Facebook account;
2. Holden has a pattern of harassing others;
3. Holden has a pattern of making false complaints to MCFD, the police and the Society for the Prevention of Cruelty to Animals;
4. Holden has victimized at least a dozen people and continues to harass and threaten her victims;
5. Hanlon believes that Mrs. Holden does not have PI training;
6. Hanlon believes that Ms. Holden lied on her PI application;
7. Holden is a pathological liar;
8. Holden admitted that she had been convicted of uttering threats.

- Hanlon admits to posting the article and to updating it to add the word "allegedly" before many of the allegations made against Ms. Holden.

- Further, Mr. Hanlon admits that the article was posted on LinkedIn under the title "Gender Bias in Canada's Justice System".

- Holden submits that, despite the fact Mr. Hanlon added the word "allegedly" to many of the posts on December 13, 2016, the defamatory meaning of the words remains unaltered. Ms. Holden submits that, since the person making the allegations is Mr. Hanlon, the addition of the word "allegedly" does not change the factual nature of the statements. I agree.

Extent of the publication

- Hanlon admitted that this post had received "one or two" responses on the LinkedIn article.

- In cross-examination, Mr. Hanlon also acknowledged that the article was posted (with the text copied and pasted, rather than hyperlinked) to the Facebook profile of Global News because he "wanted the public to know what was going on". An undated screenshot of the Global News Facebook page discloses that it has over

1.7 million "likes". However, there is no evidence of how many people viewed the article on the Global News Facebook.

- Based upon the totality of the evidence, I conclude that this posting was published. I can reasonably infer that this posting was read by one or more individuals in British

g) Facebook Post: Veterans Transition Network

- In mid-May 2017, Mr. Hanlon again made a posting on Facebook regarding Ms. Holden. The post appeared on the Facebook page of the Veterans Transition Network, a group that is specific to the Vancouver-Abbotsford area, in the form of a comment. The evidence discloses that the Facebook page has over 8,600 Facebook "likes" and a similar number of page followers. The post read:

There is one company, NPL Service, INC. in Abbotsford that claims to be "Veteran Friendly" on its job posts. DO NOT BELIEVE IT!! Stay away from that company. The owner is a con artist and has allegedly scammed both clientele as well as employees. As well the owner has a violent criminal history. For further information, please do not hesitate to contact me.

- Hanlon has admitted that he was the author of the Facebook post.

Extent of the publication

- On cross-examination, Mr. Hanlon acknowledged that it was "safe to say" that someone would read what he posted in the

- Although Mr. Hanlon's comment did not generate any "likes" or comments, the original post, upon which he had commented, was "liked" nine times and "shared" 19 times.

- Based upon the totality of the evidence, I conclude that this posting was published. It can reasonably be inferred that it was read by one or more individuals in British

h) LinkedIn Article: Beware of PI Con-Artists

- On August 8, 2017, Mr. Hanlon posted a short article entitled "Beware of PI Con-Artists" on his LinkedIn profile. A link to the article was posted to a Facebook

   page called "Protecting Canadian Children" on September 4, 2017. The short article reads:
   I was recently given information about an Abbotsford private investigator who's offering anti-terrorist investigations. Unfortunately, the PI in question is not qualified to offer that type of specialized investigation.
   In fact, the PI in question is not even properly trained in any of their services, nor do they have employees that are qualified in that specialty.
   So, beware of private investigators who are con-artists. Make sure the PI you hire, is trained and qualified to offer the services they allege to provide.
   The PI in question is also linked to BC MCFD as well as the PIABC.

- Hanlon admitted on cross-examination that he posted links to this message broadly, and on multiple Facebook pages, to ensure that the public in the Lower Mainland was aware of it. As stated above, these links do not constitute de novo publication of the defamatory words.

- The original post on LinkedIn had five "likes" and a single "comment" at the time it was printed off of the

- A plaintiff must prove that an impugned publication is "of or concerning" him or her. The key question is: would the statements lead reasonable people who know the plaintiff to conclude that those statements refer to the plaintiff? The judicial test, as formulated by the Court of Appeal, is "whether the recipient would, in light of the surrounding circumstances, reasonably believe that the person referred to in the defamatory statements is the plaintiff": Weaver at para.

- Balancing the evidence as a whole, I am not persuaded that the plaintiffs have satisfied the threshold for proving that this particular publication is "of or concerning" them in the sense that reasonable people who know the plaintiffs would conclude that the publication refers to the

i) Mr. Schiele's Facebook posts

- On August 8, 2017, the notice of civil claim was filed against Mr. Hanlon and Mr. Schiele. On August 11, 2017, Mr. Schiele posted a link to the notice of civil claim, with the heading "Dianna Holden Civil suit against Google, Facebook & brainsyntax Holden's attempt to cover her tracks ..." to five Facebook groups.

- Additionally, Mr. Schiele, in a comment on his original post in Worldwide Justice and Equality Movement, posted a link to the article "Gender Bias in Canada's Justice System", at (f)

- Notably, none of Mr. Schiele's Facebook posts are included in the plaintiffs' pleadings.

- I conclude that, in light of the critical importance of pleadings in defamation actions, it would be unjust for the Court to include Mr. Schiele's Facebook posts in its

j) LinkedIn article: Freedom of Speech under Attack

- On August 21, 2017, Mr. Hanlon posted an article called "Freedom of Speech Under Attack" on LinkedIn. This article was also posted on Twitter, Facebook, Mr. Hanlon's personal website, and brainsyntax.com. I reproduce the article in its entirety:

In my last blog about the experiences I had regarding Dianna Holden, I outlined how she would make false accusations against me, then turn around and deny that she was the one harassing me, pointing the finger at an individual named Rory. I have no idea who this Rory is.

Last year, in July of 2016, Dianna Holden filed, in my opinion, a false complaint against me to the Abbotsford Police. The investigating officer, in my opinion, was manipulated by Dianna Holden into believing that her complaint was true.

The bottom line is this, in my opinion, Dianna Holden, filed the false complaint, knowing that what I stated about her in a private e-mail to Alberta private investigator Mark Gruschynski was in fact true. That is why I am accusing Dianna Holden in making a false complaint to the police.

Further, in my background investigation of Dianna Holden, I was told numerous times by those she's victimized that she would file complaints to the police and child protective services that were allegedly false complaints.

Also, during my background investigation of Dianna Holden, it was also brought to my attention that she was accused of committing fraud and extortion, as well as identifying herself as a private investigator. And that is she is not successful in one venue (i.e. criminal charges), she will pursue another venue (i.e. law suits).

...

What I don't get is this; I was a volunteer role player for Abbotsford Police for their tactical training scenarios, yet when Dianna Holden filed her false complaint, Abbotsford Police did not take into account that I was a volunteer role player for them for over 3 years. Nor did they take into account that I was in the role as a private investigator when I disclosed information to the Alberta private investigator.

...

Getting back to the section 300 false libel charge; because Crown did not approve the charge, Dianna Holden recently filed a "Notice of Civil Claim" against 7 parties, including myself (I was the first served), Facebook Inc., Google Inc., Crown Counsel (for not charging me). To protect the privacy of the unnamed defendants, their names are not included in this blog update.

Now just to touch on the history of Dianna Holden; she has been a Ms. Holden in at least 15 civil matters, and a Defendant in at least 19 civil matters. She suffers from severe mental health issues, and has allegedly conned Security Programs Division in granting her a private investigator licence. She is also known to lie and believes her lies to be true. In my opinion, based on an educated case, as well as life experiences, Dianna Holden is a sociopath. She also has a criminal history: assault, stalking, and uttering death threats, not to mention filing false complaints and harassing / intimidating those who either step forward as a witness, or those who attempt to fight back against her.

- Hanlon admits that he authored this article, and that he posted it on LinkedIn. He also posted the article to brainsyntax.com. However, there is no evidence before the Court as to whether the posting to brainsyntax.com was in the form of a hyperlink, or whether the defamatory words themselves were posted to brainsyntax.com.

- Further, on August 22, 2017, Mr. Hanlon posted a link to this article to the Facebook group Canada Court Watch. Mr. Hanlon followed his post to the Canada Court Watch group with a post of the first "Freedom of Speech" article, at (f) above, to the same

- He also posted a link to this second "Freedom of Speech" article in the Facebook group Proud Boys Canada on August 26,

Extent of the publication

- Based upon the totality of the evidence I conclude that this article was published. In light of the fact that the article was published on LinkedIn and

Hanlon's personal website, it is reasonable to infer that this posting was read by one or more individuals in British Columbia

- Given that there is no evidence before the Court as to the form of the posting on brainsyntax.com, I cannot find that the defamatory words were published on brainsyntax.com. Mr. Hanlon also admitted to posting a link to the article on Twitter, which does not constitute publication. Similarly, posting a link to the article on Canada Court Watch does not constitute

- The link to the second "Freedom of Speech" article in the Facebook group Proud Boys Canada had 31 "views" and two "likes", as of September 29, 2017. This does not constitute cogent evidence that an individual has followed the link and read the alleged defamatory statements and therefore does not constitute publication of the alleged defamatory statements: see Malak at para.

1. **Facebook Post: Comment on Canada Court Watch**

- On August 26, 2017, Mr. Hanlon posted a comment on the Canada Court Watch Facebook group, as follows:

One observer to note and be extremely careful of is an individual named Dianna Holden, who, in my opinion, scammed the BC government in granting her a private investigator licence and a security business licence so she can conduct services as an Access Observer (she has also allegedly set up unsuspecting parents who are dealing with MCFD). Bottom line, beware of NPL Services Inc and NPL Services Ltd (aka National People Locator) in the Abbotsford, BC area. She's also extremely litigious (look her up on CSO civil and criminal searches). she's very well known for slandering others and for accusing others of slandering her (even though what is said about her is the truth, yet what she says about others is not). It also seems that those she has victimized as afraid to defend themselves against her. however, I seem to be the only one who does not fear her (but then I was an Army Drill Instructor and have a legal background)! whoever is reading this, if you've been victimized by Dianna Holden, and are not afraid to share your story via a sworn statement (aka: Affidavit) private message me via facebook.

- *Hanlon admits to being the author of this post, and to posting it on Facebook.*

Extent of the publication

- *Hanlon acknowledged that the Facebook post has one "like", but does not know who this was.*

- *Based upon the totality of the evidence, I conclude that this posting was published. It is reasonable to infer that this posting was read by one or more individuals in British*

l) *Article posted on personal website: "Intimidation Tactics of Dianna Holden"*

- On September 4, 2017, Mr. Hanlon posted an article on his personal website entitled "Intimidation Tactics of Dianna Holden". The article reads as follows:

    Recently, Dianna Holden, a mentally unstable con-artist filed a Notice of Civil Claim against seven parties: Lee Hanlon (that would be me), Patricia Pelley, Lorelei Edwards, Facebook, Inc. Google, Inc., Her Majesty the Queen as represented by the Assistant Deputy Attorney, Criminal Justice Branch (aka: BC Crown Prosecutors), Vincent Schiele.
    Holden also listed NPL Services, Inc., and National People Locator as plaintiffs. Dianna Holden has a habit of intimidating those who fight back against her. If you read my other articles (posted her on LinkedIn) you will see that Dianna Holden has been harassing me on and off since December 2011.
    Now because Dianna Holden has included me in her latest frivolous civil claim (which has no merit whatsoever!), I am fighting back. First to seek an Injunction preventing her from further abusing the judicial system (meaning for her to pursue a future claim she need Leave of Court), and to have both her Security Worker Licence and Security Business Licence revoked, and to have both her businesses dissolved.
    Because I'm fighting back, Dianna Holden has made me an open target. Just recently two individual claiming to be victimizes by Dianna Holden attempted to set me up for criminal charges. Both individuals were seeking someone to physically harm Dianna Holden, and when I didn't bit, at least one of them

started threatening me and making the same false accusations that Dianna Holden made. Further, Dianna Holden also contacted one of my current employers and made false slanderous accusations about me (the very same slanderous false accusations she made in her Notice of Civil Claim).

Dianna Holden and her so-called friends MUST understand, that their intimidation tactics DO NOT WORK ON ME!!! I have put Dianna Holden on notice to cease and desist!!!!!! The texts I received will be shown to the police, and will also be brought up in court.

- Hanlon admits to authoring and posting the articles to his website, as well as to LinkedIn. He also admitted to posting it, in some form, on brainsyntax.com,

though it is unclear whether the words were posted themselves, or if this was in the form of a hyperlink. Given that there was no evidence before the Court as to the form of posting on brainsyntax.com, I cannot find that the defamatory words were published on brainsyntax.com. Mr. Hanlon also admitted to posting a link on Twitter and the Canada Court Watch Facebook group, which did not constitute publication.

- The article was "shared" once on LinkedIn, but Mr. Hanlon admitted on cross-examination that he was the one who had "shared"

- The link posted to the Canada Court Watch Facebook group, had four "reactions", and various comments from individuals other than Mr. Hanlon. Although the post was in the form of a hyperlink, it is reasonable to infer that at least one of the commenting individuals clicked on the link prior to commenting upon the post. This constitutes a further level of engagement than executing a "like" on Facebook. In all the circumstances, it is reasonable to infer that at least one individual who commented upon the post followed the link, and thus read the article

- Based upon the totality of the evidence, I conclude that this article was published. It is reasonable to infer that this article was read by one or more individuals in British

m) Post on personal website: "Criminal Harassment (AKA Stalking) Laws in Canada"

- On September 11, 2017, Mr. Hanlon wrote a post on his personal website entitled "Criminal Harassment (AKA Stalking) Laws in Canada". After listing numerous manners by which one may be "stalked" (in Mr. Hanlon's opinion), the article continues:

In my case, the stalker is Dianna Holden, also known as Leigh Holden, Myrtle Higginbottoms, Laura Godard, Tamra

Samuels (claiming to be a Penticton Lawyer). Then there is Leonard and Gary – Leonard was fishing for information, then asked if I wanted to cause physical harm to Dianna Holden, and then made remarks that was misinformation; Gary wanted me to cause physical harm to Dianna Holden, and when I refused, Gary became extremely abusive, and made the very same false accusations that Dianna Holden has made as an unknown facebook user and as Tamra Samuels.

Dianna Holden made a false complaint to Abbotsford Police, unfortunately, as APD, in my opinion aren't properly trained in recognizing and conducting

investigations related to Stalking (aka: Criminal Harassment), they bought into Dianna Holden's false complaint. The complaint was related to the criminal offense of false libel. APD conducted the investigation and submitted a section 300 *(false libel) charge to the Abbotsford Crown. Abbotsford Crown did their due diligence and did not approve the APD charge recommendation.

That angered Dianna Holden, so what she did next was file a false complaint to Security Programs division. SPD determined that I did not violate the Security Services Act, or Regulations, and advised Dianna Holden that I have a right to free speech (section 2 of the Canadian Charter of Rights and Freedoms). Again, Dianna Holden became extremely angry.

Flash forward one year. On August 8, 2017 Dianna Holden filed a notice of Civil claim, making unfounded and false accusations against 7 Defendants: Lee Hanlon (that would be this writer); Facebook, Inc.; Google Inc; Her Majesty The Queen, as the Assistant Deputy Attorney General, the Criminal Justice Branch; Vincent Schiele, and two more parties, who've also been victimized by Dianna Holden.

Since Dianna Holden received a copy of my Form 2 Response, she has harassed me via text messages (on my cell phone) as Leonard and Gary, called on of my employers and made false and slanderous accusations about me, followed up with an e-mail to my employer, threatening him with civil action because he hired me, e-mailing me with false and slanderous accusations, blaming me for the loss of one of her security contracts, posting false and slanderous comments on LinkedIn, and causing me to lose a LinkedIn connection when she posted a slanderous comment the night she had me served with her Notice of Civil Claim.

Dianna Holden conducted herself in the above manner with the intent of intimidating me to give in to her false and slanderous Civil claim. And her anger intensified only because she is unable to intimidate me or cause my employer to terminate my employment.

...

Being a Stalking victim is not a pleasant experience, especially when the victim is male, and the accused stalker is female who suffers from mental health issues, and delusions that they have an above board professional reputation.

And it doesn't help when the accused stalker also has a violent criminal history. And it doesn't help when the accused female stalker allegedly conned Security Programs in granting them a private investigator licence and a Security Business Licence.

Now that accused female stalker can use their private investigator, and private investigation business status to continue stalking their victims.

The accused female stalker has used the judicial system numerous times in targeting victims. CSO shows the accused female stalker has filed at least 15 law suites since 1996. This must stop! It seems that I may be the only one willing to address that matter with the courts. Even the Response from the Criminal Justice Branch calls the actions of Dianna Holden abusive regarding her use of the judicial system.

...

- Hanlon admits to being the author of the article and to posting the article on Twitter, LinkedIn, and Brainsyntax.

- The evidence clearly establishes that the article was published on LinkedIn. However, it is not established on the evidence whether the post to Twitter and to brainsyntax.com were publications de novo of the impugned statements, or whether they were in the form of a

Extent of the publication

- The article was shared at least three times on LinkedIn. In addition, Mr. Hanlon posted a link to the article to Canada Court Watch. The post to Canada Court Watch was "liked" six times, "shared" three times, and commented on by two individuals (with replies to each).

- It is not established on the evidence as to whether the Twitter page generated any views, although Mr. Hanlon has over 250 followers on Twitter and he re-tweeted and liked his own

- Based upon the totality of the evidence I conclude that this article was published. It is reasonable to infer that this posting was read by one or more individuals in British

n) Facebook Post: Family Support Group for those and their Families Dealing with Xyolhemeylh

- On September 14, 2017, Mr. Hanlon copied and pasted something that Ms. Holden had previously written into a Facebook group called "Family Support Group for those and their Families Dealing with Xyolhemeylh", a Fraser Valley-

based Indigenous child and family services society. Mr. Hanlon added the following introductory comments to the posted text:

Interesting that Dianna Holden claims to defend Freedom of Speech when she and others allegedly exposed the actions of government social workers yet when the unethical actions of Dianna Holden and her businesses are exposed, she will take you to court, and she will also attempt to intimidate you if you fight back!!

- *Hanlon has admitted to posting the statement in the group.*

Extent of the publication

- *I conclude that this posting was published. The evidence did not disclose any views or likes, and there is no evidence before the Court as to the number of members in the group. Nonetheless, given the nature of a Facebook group dedicated to the subject of an agency in British Columbia, it can reasonably be inferred that Mr. Hanlon's comments were read by one or more individuals in British Columbia.*

ISSUES

- *I will analyze the issues under the following headings:*

- *Claim in defamation against:*

- *Hanlon;*

- *Schiele;*

- *What, if any, damages should be awarded to the plaintiffs?*

- *Should a permanent injunction be issued?*

- Hanlon has admitted, in both the notice to admit and at trial, that he wrote and posted each statement that the plaintiffs allege is defamatory. Due to the numerous allegedly defamatory statements contained within each individual posting or article, and the repetitive nature of some of the statements, I will enumerate and analyze the defamatory statements, rather than the individual posting or article. This is the most coherent manner to deal with the legal analysis. I will also identify where the plaintiffs' submissions did not adhere to the issues raised in the pleadings.

CHARTER DEFENCE

- In their respective pleadings, Mr. Hanlon and Mr. Schiele each invoke s. 2(b) of the *Canadian Charter of Rights and Freedoms*, Part I of the *Constitution Act, 1982*, being Schedule B to the *Canada Act 1982* (U.K.), 1982, c. 11 [*Charter*], as a defence to the plaintiffs' claim in

- The relevant section of the *Charter* provides as follows:

1.   Everyone has the following fundamental freedoms:

...

(b) freedom of thought, belief, opinion and expression, including freedom of the press and other media of communication;

...

- I do not accept that the constitutional rights of the defendants to freedom of expression affords them the right to defame. This proposition finds no coherent support in the

- I adopt the following analysis from the Ontario Court of Appeal in *Lewis v. Rancourt*, 2015 ONCA 513 at para. 17:

[17] We do not accept the appellant's submission that his constitutional right to freedom of expression affords him the

right to defame. First, the appellant has led no evidence or argument that the respondent's legal proceeding is a government action that would engage the Charter. Second, while the Supreme Court has modified the common law of defamation (see Hill v. Church of Scientology, 1995 CanLII 59 (SCC), [1995] 2 S.C.R. 1130; Grant v. Torstar, 2009 SCC 61 (CanLII), [2009] 3 S.C.R. 640)) the appellant has failed to bring himself within any Charter-based defence. In the first sentence of Mair, Binnie J. wrote for the majority of the Supreme Court , "the defence of fair comment.......... helps hold the balance in the law of defamation between two

fundamental values, namely the respect for individuals and protection of their reputation from unjustified harm on the one hand, and on the other hand, the

freedom of expression and debate that is said to be the 'very life blood of our

freedom and free institutions'". Rather than attempting to prove that his right

to freedom of expression should, at law, overcome the respondent's right to protect her reputation, the appellant refused to participate in the trial.

[Emphasis added.]

- First, the defendants have not established that the plaintiffs' legal proceeding is a government action that would engage the Charter. The Supreme Court of Canada McKinney v. University of Guelph, [1990] 3 S.C.R. 229, underscored the significance of the limitation on the application of the Charter to actions of government. La Forest J. provided the following instructive distillation of the animating principles at page 262:

The exclusion of private activity from the Charter was not a result of happenstance. It was a deliberate choice which must be respected. We do not really know why this approach was taken, but several reasons suggest themselves. Historically, bills of rights, of which that of the Unites States is

the great constitutional exemplar, have been directed at government. Government is the body that can enact and enforce rules and authoritatively impinge on individual freedom. Only government requires to be constitutionally shackled to preserve the rights of the individual. ...

- Second, there has been no principled legal basis advanced on which to conclude that, in all the circumstances of this case, the defendants' right to freedom of expression should overcome the plaintiffs' right to protect their respective reputations.

- In sum, I conclude that s. 2(b) of the Charter cannot be invoked as a defence to the plaintiffs' claim.

LEGAL FRAMEWORK

- *I previously summarized the governing principles in Lougheed Estate v. Wilson, 2017 BCSC 1366, rev'd in part 2018 BCCA 441 [Lougheed Estate]. I adopt that summary*

- *The law of defamation seeks to protect the worth and value of an individual's reputation without unduly inhibiting freedom of*

- *To establish a prima facie case in defamation, the plaintiffs need only establish threeelements:*

1. *the words or phrases were defamatory, in the sense that they would tend to lower the plaintiffs' reputation in the eyes of a reasonable person;*

1. *the words referred to the plaintiffs; and*

1. *the words were published, in that they were communicated to at least one person other than the*

- Once these elements are established on a balance of probabilities, the law presumes the words are false and that the plaintiff has suffered damage: Grant v. Torstar Corp., 2009 SCC 61 [Grant].

Were the statements defamatory?

- Not every criticism of a person or disparaging comment is defamatory. A defamatory statement is one that has a tendency to lower the reputation of the person to whom it refers in the estimation of right-thinking members of society generally and, in particular, to cause him or her to be regarded with feelings of hatred, contempt, ridicule, fear, dislike or disesteem. The test is an objective one: Color Your World Corp. v. Canadian Broadcasting Corp. (1998), 38 O.R. (3d) 97 (C.A.) at para. 15. The Court of Appeal outlined the right-thinking person standard as follows:

[15] The standard of what constitutes a reasonable or ordinary member of the public is difficult to articulate. It should not be so low as to stifle free expression unduly, nor so high as to imperil the ability to protect the integrity of a person's reputation. The impressions about the content of any broadcast
- or written statement - should be assessed from the perspective of someone reasonable, that is, a person who is reasonably thoughtful and informed, rather than someone with an overly fragile sensibility. A degree of common sense must be attributed to viewers.

- *Whether a statement is defamatory is to be determined from the natural and ordinary meaning of the words. Moreover, the publication containing the impugned statement must be considered as a whole. The traditional axiom is that "the bane and the antidote must be taken together", that is, a statement taken out of context may be considered defamatory but its "sting" may be neutralized by another part of the*

- *Words may convey a defamatory meaning literally, inferentially or by legal innuendo. A literal meaning is a direct conveyance, where as an inferential meaning or a legal innuendo have their meaning conveyed based upon extrinsic facts: Weaver at para.*

- *Madam Justice Dickson, at para. 72 of Weaver, summarized the analytical difference between literal meaning and inferential or legal innuendo as follows:*

[72] Where the literal meaning of words is in issue, it is unnecessary to go beyond the words themselves to prove that they are defamatory. Where a claim is based on the inferential meaning of words, the question is one of impression: what would the ordinary person infer from the words in the context in which they were used? Both literal and inferential defamatory

meaning reside within the words, as part of their natural and ordinary meaning. In contrast, where legal innuendo is pleaded the impugned words take on defamatory meaning from outside circumstances beyond general knowledge, but known to the recipient.

- The meaning of multiple publications may be understood together in certain circumstances. For example, "if one publication is referenced in or otherwise closely connected to another publication, depending on the pleadings, issues and circumstances of the case, it may be appropriate to read them together to ascertain their combined meaning": Weaver at para.

Did the statements refer to the plaintiffs?

- As I referred to earlier, the plaintiffs must prove a factual question, on the balance of probabilities, that the statements are "of or concerning" them: Booth v. British Columbia Television Broadcasting System (1982), 139 D.L.R. (3d) 88 at 92 (B.C.C.A.).

Publication

- I have set out the governing principles regarding publication earlier in these Reasons at paras.59-66.

Defences

- Once the court finds a statement to be prima facie defamatory, the onus then shifts to the defendant to advance a defence that would justify publication of the defamatory statement. Because of the low threshold required of the plaintiff, most defamation actions turn on the applicability of one of the

- Different potential defences are available depending whether the impugned statement is fact or opinion. Statements of fact can be defended as truth (justification) or public interest responsible communication, while opinion is generally defended as fair comment. Both statements of fact and of opinion may attract the defence of

- For this reason, it is important to determine whether the defamatory statement is fact or

- The Supreme Court discussed what constitutes "comment" in WIC Radio

1. Simpson, 2008 SCC 40 [WIC Radio SCC] at para. 26:

... "comment" includes a "deduction, inference, conclusion, criticism, judgment, remark or observation which is generally incapable of proof". Brown's The Law of Defamation in Canada (2nd ed. (loose-leaf)) cites ample authority for the proposition that words that may appear to be statements of fact may, in pith and substance, be properly construed as comment. This is particularly so in an editorial context where loose, figurative or hyperbolic language is used (Brown, vol. 4, at p. 27-317) in the context of political debate, commentary, media campaigns and public discourse. See also, R. D. McConchie and D. A. Potts, Canadian Libel and Slander Actions (2004), at p. 340.

- Whether a statement is fact or comment must be determined from the perspective of a reasonable viewer or reader: WIC Radio SCC at para.

- In this case both defendants have pleaded only the defence of

- The defence of justification simply means that the impugned statement is substantially true. The burden is on the defendant to prove substantial truth on a balance of probabilities. Madam Justice Adair instructively expounded the test for justification in *Casses v. Canadian Broadcasting Corp.*, 2015 BCSC 2150 at para. 550:

[550] Justification is an absolute defence to defamation. It applies to statements of fact. It will succeed if the defendant proves, on a balance of probabilities, the truth of what is alleged to be defamatory. However, what is required to be proven is not the truth of each and every word or the literal truth of the statement. Rather, a defendant must only prove on a balance of probabilities that the gist or sting of the defamation was true, and it is sufficient if the defendant proves that a defamatory expression was substantially true. Minor inaccuracies do not preclude a defence of justification so long as the publication conveyed an accurate impression. The test is whether the defamatory expression, as published, would have a different effect on a reader or listener than what the pleaded truth would have produced. See *Cimolai v. Hall*, at paras. 171-173; *Wilson v. Switlo*, 2011 BCSC 1287, at paras. 440-441; and *Jay v. Hollinger Canadian Newspapers*, 2002 BCSC 1840, at para. 4.

- As noted, the defence of justification turns on the sting of the impugned statement and whether it would have a different effect on a reader than the truth; see also *Jay v. Hollinger Canadian Newspapers*, 2002 BCSC 1655 at para. 53, where

McEwan J. stated that justification can only be assessed by comparing the sting of the published words with the effect of the actual facts.

- The repetition rule is especially important to the defence of justification. That rule holds that a defendant cannot defend a defamation action on the basis that he or she has simply repeated what someone else has said. As the English Court of Appeal explained the principle in Roberts v. Gable, [2007] EWCA 721 at

paras. 54-55:

- The repetition rule is well-established and has an important place in libel law. The rule was succinctly described by Lord Reid in Lewis v Daily Telegraph Ltd [1964] A.C. 234, 236 as:

"Repeating someone else's libellous statement is just as bad as making the statement directly."
Indeed it may be much worse:
"... if the words had not been repeated by the newspaper, the damage done by J. [by slandering the plaintiff] would be as nothing compared to the damage done by this newspaper when it repeated it. It broadcast the statement to the people at large ..." Truth (N.Z.) Ltd v Holloway [1960] 1 W.L.R. 997, 1003 PC.

- Thus the rule is that if A makes a defamatory statement about B and C repeats it, C cannot succeed in the defence of *justification by showing that A made the statement: C must prove the charge against B is true. This is so even if C believes the statement to be true and even when C names A as his source. Lord Devlin put it succinctly in Lewis v Daily Telegraph at p. 284: "For the purposes of the law of libel a hearsay statement is the same as a direct statement, and that is all there is to "*

- Accordingly, it is not open to a defendant who republishes a defamatory allegation to assert that it is true that the allegation was made; rather, he is in the same position as the originator of the allegation and must prove its

- The Supreme Court emphasized the importance of the repetition rule in the internet era when defamatory statements "can be reproduced electronically with the speed of a few keystrokes": Grant at paras. 114,

- In Taseko Mines Ltd. v. Western Canada Wilderness Committee, 2016 BCSC 109, rev'd in part 2017 BCCA 431, Mr. Justice Funt stated at para. 21, that "facts arising before or after the publication may be used by the defence" to establish the defence of justification (citing Cohen v. Daily Telegraph Ltd., [1968] 1 W.L.R. 916 at

919 (C.A.)). Therefore, facts that have come to Mr. Hanlon's attention after the posting of the defamatory statements, if properly adduced in evidence, are available to establish justification.

ANALYSIS

(a) Claim against Mr. Hanlon

Position of the Parties

- Holden's primary contention is that, by virtue of their literal or inferential meanings, each of the impugned statements enumerated in her pleadings are defamatory.

- For his part, Mr. Hanlon does not dispute that the impugned statements were defamatory. Rather, as a complete answer to the plaintiffs' claim, he relies on the defence of

- *Holden counters with the submission that Mr. Hanlon has not established on a balance of probabilities that the impugned statements are substantially true. She asserts that, on the authorities, even if Mr. Hanlon honestly believed the statements to be true, this is insufficient to prove a defence of justification. Further, Ms. Holden underscores that, while Mr. Hanlon may have been repeating statements that he was told by third parties, he must nonetheless establish that the statements were substantially true. As I stated earlier, this is commonly referred to as the repetition rule.*

The Allegedly Defamatory Statements

- At the outset, I identify the alleged defamatory statements that were raised at trial that were not included in the plaintiffs' pleadings:

- Holden does not respect privacy laws or client confidentiality;

- NPL is not "veteran friendly".

- In light of their omission from the pleadings and based upon the Weaver

principles, those statements are not actionable.

- I turn to address the impugned words and expressions referred to in the pleadings.

- Given the number of the alleged defamatory statements, I have analyzed them in subject matter

- To reiterate, the judicial test of what constitutes a defamatory statement is one which has a tendency to injure the reputation of the person to whom it refers and to lower him or her in the estimation of right-thinking members of society generally. An ordinary, right-thinking member of society is someone "who is reasonably thoughtful and informed, rather than someone with an overly fragile sensibility": Bou Malhab v. Diffusion Métromédia CMR inc., 2011 SCC 9 at para. 36. A degree of common sense must be attributed to

- With respect to meaning, the court's role is to objectively determine what a reasonable and right-thinking reader would have understood from the words that were published.

The determination of the meanings anchors the analysis because it frames what must be proven under the various pleaded

- Earlier in these Reasons, I found that each of the impugned statements set out below was published and was read by one or more individuals in British Columbia. The next question is whether they were

- I also find that each of these statements refer to Ms. Holden. In the analysis that follows, I have indicated whenever the impugned statements may refer to any one of corporate plaintiffs in addition to Ms. Holden. The context in which the alleged defamatory statements are made is key. I have considered the literal and inferential meanings of each of the impugned statements in the immediate context in which they were

(i) Ms. Holden is a liar / displays pathological tendencies / displays sociopathiccharacteristics

- These allegedly defamatory statements appear in the following postings:

- Personal website article (cross-posted to Global News) at (f);

- LinkedIn article (cross-posted to Facebook) at (j); and

- Personal website article (cross-posted to various websites) at (m).

- In my view, the natural and ordinary meaning of the impugned words are defamatory in their literal sense in so far as they allege that Ms. Holden's dishonesty is so pervasive that she is a pathological liar. This infers that she has been diagnosed as such. The inferential meaning of the words she "displays sociopathic characteristics" connotes an individual who has an antisocial personality who lacks empathy or remorse for her unethical behaviour and often breaks rules and makes impulsive decisions. I am satisfied the allegations and imputations would tend to lower the reputation of Ms. Holden in the eyes of a reasonable

- Hanlon stated that, based upon his one year of psychology and one year of sociology, he believes that Ms. Holden is displaying pathological tendencies and sociopathic characteristics. He describes this as a "layman's assessment". He further contends the fact that Ms. Holden denies having had harassed him supports a finding that his statements Ms. Holden is a pathological liar are true.

- Hanlon also points to a Craigslist ad posting for the position of director of security operations. When he responded to the posting and inquired about the position, he was told in an email that it would be an asset for an applicant to be able to handle a team of 780 guards. Mr. Hanlon subsequently identified the advertising company as NPL Services Inc. Mr. Hanlon submits that this job posting shows that Ms. Holden is a pathological liar. I am not persuaded that this response regarding a job advertisement establishes that the Ms. Holden is a liar or displays pathological tendencies. It merely states the qualifications in an employee that Ms. Holden, in her capacity as an employer, was seeking. In the absence of any cogent evidence on the point, the Court cannot speculate on the explanation for thestatement.

- The totality of the evidence does not support a finding that Ms. Holden has ever been diagnosed either as a pathological liar or as displaying sociopathic characteristics.

- Balancing the evidence as a whole, I find that Mr. Hanlon has failed to prove on a balance of probabilities, that the gist or sting of these impugned words is

- If I am incorrect and these statements constitute subjective assessments incapable of proof the defence of justification is inapplicable, Although Mr. Hanlon has not pleaded fair comment, I add for completeness that these statements do not qualify as fair comment. I reviewed the animating principles for fair comment in Lougheed Estate at paras. 193-200 and 208-211.These statements referred to above are not comment on matter of public interest nor are they based on a factual foundation that has been proved to be "substantially true".

(ii) Ms. Holden is a con artist / fraud / fraudulently obtained her PI license / does not have experience to provide the services she offers (the "PI allegations")

- This allegedly defamatory statements appear in the following postings:

- Craigslist posting at (b);

- Facebook posts at (c);

- Personal website article (cross-posted to Global News) at (f);

- Facebook post at (g);

- LinkedIn article (cross-posted to various websites) at (j);

- Facebook post at (k);

- Personal website article (cross-posted to various websites) at (l); and

- Personal website article (cross-posted to various websites) at (m).

- I am satisfied that the natural and ordinary meanings of the impugned PI allegations, in both their literal sense and their inferential meaning, are defamatory, as they allege that Ms. Holden is dishonest, acts fraudulently, defrauded her regulator, and lacks the requisite skills and training to be a private investigator. The allegations connote unlawful and unethical behaviour on the part of Ms. Holden. I am

    satisfied that these allegations and imputations would tend to lower the reputation of Ms. Holden in the eyes of a reasonable person. These are serious allegations against an individual who is seeking to establish a reputation as a trustworthy and reliable private investigator.

- In order to support his assertions, Mr. Hanlon stated that:

- in his view, the writing skills exhibited in the application for a PI equivalency licence are "way too skilled" to be the those of Ms. Holden;

- Holden misrepresented her work experience on her application;

- Holden does not perform skip-tracing activities ethically; and

- the letters Ms. Holden included in her application contained false information.

- With respect to his contention that Ms. Holden does not have the requisite experience, training or education to qualify as a private investigator, Mr. Hanlon relies upon statements from various individuals who did not testify at

Mr. Hanlon also relies upon the statements of several individuals, who did not testify at trial, who told him they had been defrauded by Ms. Holden. He admits that he took no other steps, other than speaking to these unidentified individuals, to confirm the truth of these statements. As I repeatedly cautioned Mr. Hanlon, the statements of these individuals who did not testify at trial constitute hearsay evidence and therefore were not properly admissible at trial to prove the truth of the statements.

- Hanlon admitted on cross-examination that he has no objective evidence that the information in Ms. Holden's application was false, but resolutely maintained his belief that it was, indeed, false. Furthermore, he admitted, on cross-examination, that he did not know if Ms. Holden had taken any courses in pursuit of her licence. In cross-examination, Mr.

Hanlon stated that "from what [he] gathered and observed, she isn't qualified" to provide the services she offers as a private investigator.

- Holden categorically denies the truth of these statements.

- It is not in dispute that Ms. Holden was issued a valid licence from the governing regulatory authority in B.C. Ms. Holden, who completed the basic security training course at the Justice Institute, maintains that she properly obtained her private investigator licence based upon both her training and work

- With respect to the allegation that Ms. Holden lacks the requisite training and experience, Ms. Holden submits that the requirements under the SSA, the Regulation, and the Policies provide an objective standard of experience required to obtain a private investigator's licence. Therefore, Ms. Holden maintains that the requisite "experience to offer the services she offers" is objectively

- Importantly, Ms. Holden was issued a private investigator licence by the governing regulatory body in B.C., who accepted that she had the requisite qualifications. Mr. Hanlon made a complaint about Ms. Holden to the regulatory body for private investigators in B.C. It is common ground that the complaint was dismissed. Mr. Hanlon admitted in his pleading that the regulator found the complaints unfounded. In any case, there was no reliable evidence that the regulatory body has taken any action to suspend or remove Ms. Holden's private investigator

- On the totality of the evidence, Mr. Hanlon has failed to prove on a balance of probabilities that the gist or sting of the impugned PI allegations were true. The evidence falls short of establishing that Ms. Holden is a fraud and fraudulently obtained her private investigator licence. Nor is it established that she lacks the requisite experience to provide private investigation

- I am not persuaded that the defence of justification applies to the defamatory statement that Ms. Holden is a "con artist" because that is a subjective assessment incapable of proof. I add for completeness that the statement does not qualify as fair comment. Mr. Hanlon's "con artist" comment is not on a matter of public interest nor is it based on a factual foundation that has been proved to be "substantially true".

(iii)   Ms. Holden guarantees a refund if she is unsuccessful, but does not refund her fees / scams her clients

- This allegedly defamatory statement appears in the following postings:

- Email to private investigator at (a);

- Craigslist posting at (b); and

- Facebook post on the Veterans Transition Network at (g).

- The natural and ordinary meaning of the impugned words are, in their literal sense, defamatory in so far as they allege that Ms. Holden is dishonest, unethical, defrauds her clients, and engages in unfair practices. I am satisfied that these allegations would tend to lower the reputation of the plaintiffs in the eyes of a reasonable

- *Hanlon acknowledged that he had never been personally defrauded or scammed by Ms. Holden. Mr. Hanlon relies on inadmissible hearsay evidence of individuals who were not called as witnesses at trial to substantiate these statements.*

- *Holden denies the truth of these statements. Ms. Holden candidly described her fee structure to the Court and she explained that as a private investigator, she charges for time spent, rather than based on results.*

- *I find that Mr. Hanlon has not proved on a balance of probabilities that the gist or sting of these impugned statements is*

(iv)   Ms. Holden drafted a service agreement that no "credible PI" would draft / gives "my profession" a bad name

- This allegedly defamatory statement appears in the following posting:

- *Facebook posts at (c).*

- Both the inferential meaning and the natural and ordinary meaning of the impugned words, in their literal sense, are defamatory in so far as the words allege that Ms. Holden is notoriously disreputable, unskilled as a private investigator, and

engages in unfair practices. I am satisfied that the allegations and imputations would tend to lower the reputation of Ms. Holden in the eyes of a reasonable person.

- I find that the defence of justification does not apply to these defamatory statements because the statements are subjective assessments incapable of

- For completeness, I add that these statements do not qualify as fair comment. In this case, Mr. Hanlon is not commenting on a matter of public interest. Moreover, his comments are not based on a factual foundation that has been proved to be substantially

(v)   Ms. Holden is purporting to be a lawyer / harassed Mr. Hanlon with a false Facebook account / Law Society forced her to delete the account / sexually harassed Mr. Hanlon with a false Facebook account / has been harassing Mr. Hanlon since December 2011 / has a history of harassing others

- These alleged defamatory statements appear in the following postings:

- Facebook posts at (c);

- Brainsyntax article at (d);

- LinkedIn article (cross-posted to various websites) at (e);

- Personal website article (cross-posted to Global News) at (f);

- Personal website article (cross-posted to various websites) at (l); and

- Personal website article (cross-posted to various websites) at (m).

- The natural and ordinary meaning of the impugned words are, in their literal sense, defamatory as they allege that Ms. Holden wrongfully impersonated a lawyer on Facebook for which the Law Society took action. This connotes dishonest and immoral conduct. Further, the plain meaning of the other impugned statements is that she has been inappropriately harassing, including sexual harassing, Mr. Hanlon since December 2011 and that she has harassed others. This connotes that Ms. Holden repeatedly engaged in improper and threatening conduct. I am satisfied that

these allegations would tend to lower the reputation of Ms. Holden in the eyes of a reasonable person.

- Holden admitted that for purposes of obtaining access to a closed Facebook group named "United Victims of Dianna (Davidson Holden)" she created a false Facebook profile under the name Tamara Samuels and that she chose "legal community" as her occupation. She explained that that Facebook listed this occupation as "lawyer" and she did not know how to change it. She did not do this intentionally. Moreover, in the course of their correspondence, "Tamara" stated clearly to Mr. Hanlon that she was not a lawyer. She explained that she wanted access to the group to see if there was any information that was being circulated about her that would potentially threaten her personal security. I accept her explanation.

- I have not overlooked the message exchange that she had with Mr. Hanlon as Tamara Samuels in September 2016. The exchange made in an apparent effort to provoke him was inappropriate. However, I am not persuaded that this single exchange constituted harassment, a term that a reasonable reader would understand requires a pattern of repeated

- Hanlon also maintains that Ms. Holden sent him inappropriate messages as "Myrtle Higginbottoms" by way of a false Facebook account in 2011. He maintains, without any cogent evidence to support his assertions that, that the unknown "Myrtle Higginbottoms" had listed the same birthdate as Ms. Holden on his or her Facebook profile. The evidence adduced is insufficient to establish the identity of an unknown individual behind these unsolicited Facebook messages. Balancing the evidence as a whole, I am not persuaded that Mr. Hanlon established that it was Ms. Holden who sent him Facebook messages as "Myrtle Higginbottoms" in 2011. Nor was it established on the evidence that Ms. Holden was the unidentified Facebook user that sent Mr. Hanlon threatening messages in 2011, as is alleged by Mr. Hanlon.

- Hanlon admitted on cross-examination that he was not in contact with Ms. Holden from December 2011 until early 2016, but maintained that he believes Ms. Holden had been "cyberstalking" him during this time.

- With respect to Mr. Hanlon's statements that Ms. Holden has a history of harassing others, he relied upon what he had been told by other individuals who did not testify at trial. Mr. Hanlon cannot rely on these hearsay statements to establish the factual basis for the purposes of grounding a defence of

- Balancing the evidence as a whole, I conclude that Mr. Hanlon has not established that the sting or gist of any of these impugned statements is substantially

(vi)   Ms. Holden appropriates money from her company

- *This allegedly defamatory statement appears in the following postings:*

- *Craigslist posting at (b).*

- *I am satisfied that the natural and ordinary meaning of the impugned statement, in its literal sense, is defamatory in so far as it connotes that Ms. Holden is untrustworthy. The impugned statement imputes illegal conduct. The allegation and imputation would tend to lower the reputation of Ms. Holden in the eyes of a reasonable*

- *Hanlon also purports to rely on information from unknown sources that Canada Revenue Agency audited Ms. Holden and "found her doing things that were not ethical". He admits that he has no documentary evidence whatsoever to support this allegation. In the circumstances, I cannot accord any weight to Mr. Hanlon's evidence on this point.*

- *Hanlon also acknowledges that owing taxes to the Canada Revenue Agency does not necessarily amount to fraud. Indeed, even if Ms. Holden has outstanding tax debt, this does not amount to defrauding the Canada Revenue Agency;*

rather, it makes one a debtor to the Canada Revenue Agency.

- Holden explained to the Court that she is entitled to dividends as the sole shareholder and director of her company. I accept her evidence on this point.

- On the totality of the evidence, Mr. Hanlon has not proven on a balance of probabilities that the sting of this defamatory statement is substantially

(vii) Ms. Holden has mental health issues / is delusional / is mentally unstable

- This allegedly defamatory statement appears in the following postings:

- Craigslist posting at (b);

- Facebook posts at (c);

- *Brainsyntax article at (d);*

- *LinkedIn Article at (e);*

- *Personal website article (cross-posted to Global News) at (f);*

- *LinkedIn article (cross-posted to various websites) at (j);*

- *Personal website article (cross-posted to various websites) at (l); and*

- *Personal website article (cross-posted to various websites) at (m).*

- *I am not persuaded that the statement that Ms. Holden has mental health issues is defamatory in the sense that the* statements would tend to lower the reputation of Ms. Holden in the eyes of a reasonable person. The modern view is that having mental health issues is an illness that should not bear a negative

- However, the consideration of the statement that Ms. Holden is delusional and mentally unstable requires a more nuanced approach. On a contextual analysis, a reasonable reader would understand, or infer, that Ms. Holden has faulty judgment, acts irrationally, and is prone to being unbalanced and deranged. I find this factual assertion to be defamatory; the imputation would tend to lower the reputation of Ms. Holden in the eyes of a reasonable

- Holden was forthright in acknowledging that she was diagnosed with a mental health condition in 2009. She stated that it is managed, and that as part of her application for a private investigator licence, her family physician signed a medical condition form certifying that her illness was being managed. I accept Ms. Holden's evidence that her doctor does not require her to take medicationas

part of her management, and that her condition does not affect her ability to perform her profession, or to engage in daily activities. Ms. Holden also stated that she currently suffers from post-traumatic stress disorder, and that she previously suffered from agoraphobia in 2009, which was related to a particular incident.

- *Although Ms. Holden did not produce expert evidence or documentation of any kind regarding her various diagnoses, her evidence on this point was not challenged by Mr.*

- *In sum, I find that Mr. Hanlon has not proven on a balance of probabilities that the gist or sting of the allegation that Ms. Holden is delusional and mentally unstable is substantially*

- *If I am incorrect and the defamatory statements that Ms. Holden is delusional and mentally unstable are subjective assessments incapable of proof, it does not satisfy the legal test for fair comment. It is not a matter of public interest nor are the statements based on a factual foundation that is true. Accordingly, I conclude that Mr. Hanlon has not established any legal defence to the defamatory*

(viii)   Ms. Holden has a background of intimidation / violent criminal history / uttered a veiled death threat to Mr. Hanlon / was accused of committing extortion / she has a criminal history: assault, stalking, uttering death threats / she admitted she was convicted of uttering threats / stalked and targeted Mr. Hanlon (the "criminal allegations")

- These allegedly defamatory statements appear in the following postings:

- Facebook posts at (c);

- LinkedIn Article at (e);

- Personal website article (cross-posted to Global News) at (f);

- Facebook post at (g);

- LinkedIn article (cross-posted to various websites) at (j);

- Personal website article (cross-posted to various websites) at (l);

- Personal website article (cross-posted to various websites) at (m); and

- Facebook post at (n).

- In Austin v. Lynch, 2016 BCSC 1344 the court explained:

[63] An accusation of criminal conduct does not have to describe the crime technically in accordance with the Criminal Code. It need not even specify the offence. An allegation that a person is guilty of acts constituting a crime is sufficient (Campbell v. Cartmell (1999), 104 O.T.C. 349 (S.C.J.) at paras. 41- 42; see also Clark v. East Sooke Rural Association et al, 2004 BCSC 1120).

- In my view, the natural and ordinary meaning of the impugned words described above as the criminal allegations, in their literal sense, are defamatory in so far as they connote that Ms. Holden is a dangerous criminal, capable of violent behaviour, intimidation and issuing serious threats. I am satisfied that these allegations and imputations would tend to lower the reputation of Ms. Holden in the eyes of a reasonable person. These are very serious allegations against an individual engaged in a profession that is based on reputation and

- Regarding the violent behaviour allegations, Mr. Hanlon referred to the fact that there were three Peace Bonds applications brought against Ms. Holden, pursuant to s. 810 of the Criminal Code, on July 24, 2010. Ms. Holden candidly admitted that her involvement in a dispute with a neighbour had resulted in the application for a peace bond. Ms. Holden had two appearances related to the s. 810 peace bond, which ultimately was found to not have reasonable grounds for issuance. The applications were all dismissed. Contrary to the assertions of

Mr. Hanlon, I am not persuaded that this shows a pattern of violent behaviour. Moreover, and in any event, I accept Ms. Holden's evidence that this dispute was

disclosed to the licencing body in the course of her application for a private investigator's licence.

- In so far as having a "criminal history", Ms. Holden acknowledged that she has a previous conviction for "writing bad cheques" when she was "18 or 19". Ms. Holden's evidence, which I accept, is that she has received a pardon for this offence in 2009. To the extent Mr. Hanlon says Ms. Holden has a criminal history that is

- However, Mr. Hanlon's statements that Ms. Holden has a "violent" criminal history are unsubstantiated. The evidence does not establish that Ms. Holden has any other criminal convictions for "violent" crimes or otherwise. In particular, it is not established that Ms. Holden has any criminal convictions for uttering threats as is alleged by Mr. Hanlon. I do not accept Mr. Hanlon's evidence that Ms. Holden admitted to having been convicted for uttering threats. This improbable assertion does not accord with the preponderance of the probabilities of the case. Notably, Mr. Hanlon has not produced any objective evidence to support his

- Hanlon also tendered a notice of civil claim, which Ms. Holden filed against the Fraser Health Authority, inter alia, in which one of the pleaded facts refers to Ms. Holden being restrained by employees of the Fraser Health Authority. I can place no weight upon a notice of civil claim as the facts therein are allegations, not proven facts.

- Similarly, Mr. Hanlon maintains that a claim for extortion was brought against Ms. Holden by a woman named Victoria Filanovksy. The reasons for judgment of Judge Gulbransen of the BC Provincial Court, dated November 25, 2016, indicate that at its core the claim alleged that Ms. Holden falsely billed

Ms. Filanovksy. It was not a claim for extortion. In any event, the claim against Ms. Holden was

- In support of the criminal allegations, Mr. Hanlon relies upon conversations he had with "over a dozen" individuals who had told him that they had "been victimized" by Ms. Holden. This is hearsay evidence that is not properly admissible to prove the truth of those statements. Mr. Hanlon candidly acknowledged, in cross-examination,

that none of these individuals were willing to give evidence to substantiate their claims.

- The evidence does not establish that Ms. Holden has ever accused

Mr. Hanlon of being a killer. I found find her explanation for the February 2016 email exchange credible.

- Holden says she has never attended Mr. Hanlon's residence, nor has she communicated with him after these proceedings were commenced, except in the course of, and for purposes of, this litigation.

- Finally, Mr. Hanlon points to a printout from brainsyntax.com that shows an individual, using Ms. Holden's email, attempted to access the website numerous times. Mr. Hanlon submits that this substantiates the truth of his claim that

Ms. Holden has been stalking him, and in particular, that she has been cyberstalking him.

- The preponderance of the evidence I prefer falls short of proving that

Ms. Holden "stalked and targeted" Mr. Hanlon as he alleges or that Ms. Holden sent Mr. Hanlon threatening text messages.

- In summary, with the exception of the allegation that Ms. Holden "targeted" Mr. Hanlon, the criminal allegations are statements of fact. Balancing the evidence as a whole, I find that - except for the statement that Ms. Holden has a criminal history - Mr. Hanlon has failed to prove on a balance of probabilities that the gist or sting of these impugned words is

- For completeness, if the words are comment, based upon a subjective assessment and incapable of proof, the defence of justification is not available to Mr. Hanlon. Moreover, a defence of fair comment would not assist Mr.

Mr. Hanlon's comments are not on a matter of public interest nor are they based on a factual foundation that has been proved to be "substantially true".

- The allegation that Ms. Holden "targeted" Mr. Hanlon is comment based upon a subjective assessment and incapable of proof. Therefore, the defence of

justification is not available to Mr. Hanlon. For completeness, the targeting allegation does not qualify as fair comment. Mr. Hanlon's comment is not on a matter of public interest nor is it based on a factual foundation that has been proved to be "substantially true".

- If I am incorrect and the allegation that Ms. Holden "targeted" Mr. Hanlon is a statement of fact, Mr. Hanlon has failed to prove on a balance of probabilities that the gist of these impugned words is

(ix) Ms. Holden's behaviour shows a pattern of filing false complaints to the police, the Ministry of Child and Family Development and the Society for the Prevention of the Cruelty of Animals / manipulated the police into believing her complaint

- This allegedly defamatory statement appears in the following postings:

- Personal website article (cross-posted to Global News) at (f);

- LinkedIn Article (cross-posted to various websites) at (j);

- Facebook post at (k); and

- Personal website article (cross-posted to various websites) at (m).

- In my view, the meaning of the impugned words are defamatory in the literal sense in so far as they connote that Ms. Holden is dishonest and disreputable. The inferential meaning is that Ms. Holden victimizes vulnerable individuals by making false reports to the authorities. I am satisfied that these imputations and inferences would tend to lower the reputation of Ms. Holden in the eyes of a reasonable

- All of the statements in this category are factual with the exception of the allegation that Ms. Holden manipulated the

- Hanlon admitted that there is no evidence showing that Ms. Holden filed false complaints to the Society for the Prevention of Cruelty to Animals.

- It is common ground that the Abbotsford Police Department recommended to the Crown that charges for criminal libel be brought against Mr. Hanlon. Mr. Hanlon

cannot rely upon the fact that the Crown did not approve charges against him as establishing the truth of his statement that Ms. Holden filed false complaints to the police.

- With respect to the factual statements, I find that Mr. Hanlon has failed to prove on a balance of probabilities that the gist or sting of the impugned words are true.

- With respect to the allegation that Ms. Holden manipulated the police, this statement is incapable of proof and therefore the defence of justification cannot prevail. There is no evidence that the constable who investigated the com-

plaint was in any way influenced, improperly or otherwise, by Ms. Holden in formulating his charge recommendation to the Crown. For completeness, this allegation would not qualify as fair comment. Mr. Hanlon's comment is not on a matter of public interest nor is it based on a factual foundation that has been proved to be "substantially

true".

(x) *Ms. Holden has "set up" unsuspecting parents who are dealing with the Ministry of Children and Family Development*

- *This allegedly defamatory statement appears in the following posting:*

- *Facebook post at (k).*

- *The impugned words are defamatory. The inferential defamatory meaning is that Ms. Holden in unethical and betrays vulnerable individuals, who have reposed confidence in her, to the authorities. The inferential meaning or impression left by the words would tend to lower the reputation of Ms. Holden in the eyes of a reasonable person.*

- There is no evidence before the court to substantiate the truth of this statement. Mr. Hanlon has failed to prove on a balance of probabilities that the sting of the impugned words is

(xi) Ms. Holden has been involved in "at least 34" civil lawsuits / is extremely litigious

- This allegedly defamatory statement appears in the following postings:

- LinkedIn Article (cross-posted to various websites) at (j); and

- Facebook post at (k).

- The impugned words that "Ms. Holden has been involved in at least 34 civil lawsuits" without any context is not defamatory. Similarly, the impugned words "is extremely litigious" is not itself defamatory. It connotes that Ms. Holden is prone to engage in lawsuits. Without any context or explanation of the lawsuits, I am not persuaded that either of these statements would tend to lower the reputation of Ms. Holden in the eyes of a reasonable

- Holden acknowledged that she had been involved in a number of civil lawsuits, including personal injury claim arising from a motor vehicle accident. She also stated that she had a business failure early in her career that resulted in a number of lawsuits. There was no objective evidence tendered regarding the outcome of the lawsuits.

- For completeness, if the statements are defamatory, the evidence establishes that the gist of the statements is

Summary of Claim against Mr. Hanlon

- In summary on this issue, I conclude that, with the exception of the words that Ms. Holden has "mental health issues" and the statements set out in (xi) above, the allegedly defamatory statements enumerated above as (i) - (x) are plainly defamatory of Ms. Holden. The statements are reasonably ca-

pable of bearing a defamatory meaning in law and, in fact, have defamatory

- For the reasons outlined above, I conclude that Mr. Hanlon is not entitled to succeed in a defence of justification for the defamatory statements he published except as it relates to the statement that Ms. Holden has a criminal history and the statements referred to at (xi), if they are in fact defamatory. Having established a claim in defamation Ms. Holden is entitled to damages from Mr. Hanlon. I will address the appropriate quantum of those damages later in these

(b) Claim by the Corporate Plaintiffs

- I turn to the claim made by the corporate plaintiffs. For the reasons that follow, I am not persuaded that either corporate plaintiff has established a claim in defamation.

- In Malak at para. 25, the Court of Appeal affirmed that the question whether an individual or entity has been stung by a defamatory statement is a question of fact.

- *Although some of the publications, namely those at (b), (c), (e), (g) (k) and (l) above, mention NPL Services Inc. and/or National People Locator, I find that on a contextual analysis, a reasonable reader would conclude that the "sting" of the impugned defamatory statements was expressly directed at Ms. Holden personally. In the article that mentions NPL Services Inc. in the title (the Scam Alert article referred to at para.75), the defamatory statements do not allege any impropriety on behalf of the*

- *In the case authorities in which the corporate plaintiff was awarded damages, the statements impugned the integrity of the corporate plaintiffs, either directly or indirectly, whereas in this case, the statements clearly impugn the integrity of*

Ms. Holden personally. As a result, I find the analysis in those cases to be distinguishable.

(c) Claim against Mr. Schiele

- *As I noted earlier, the defendant Mr. Schiele did not attend trial. However, he filed a response to the notice of civil claim wherein he stated that he was relying upon the defence of justification and s. 2 of the Charter. Mr. Schiele was also* served with the notice to admit, dated July 19, 2018 (the "Notice to Admit") to which he did not

- Although it was not raised by counsel for the plaintiff, for completeness, I find that the Court has jurisdiction simpliciter over the claim against Mr. Schiele, as he has attorned to the jurisdiction. In his response to civil claim, Mr. Schiele defended the claim on its merits and did not dispute the jurisdiction of the Court over the

proceedings. Section 3 of the Court Jurisdiction and Proceedings Transfer Act,
S.B.C. 2003, c. 28, reads:

3 A court has territorial competence in a proceeding that is brought against a person only if
...

- during the course of the proceeding that person submits to the court's jurisdiction

- In Stewart v. Stewart, 2017 BCSC 1532, some of the defendants from Australia who had been served ex juris filed a substantive response to civil claim, and then proceeded to allege that the court did not have jurisdiction over the On this issue, the Court wrote:

- *I do, however, find that the Australian Defendants have attorned to this Court's jurisdiction by virtue of failing to comply with Rule 21-8(1)(c) which states:*
    - *A party who has been served with an originating pleading or petition in a proceeding, whether that service was effected in or outside British Columbia, may, after filing a jurisdictional response in Form 108,*

...

- *allege in a pleading or in a response to petition that the court does not have jurisdiction over that party in respect of the claim made against that party in the*

[Emphasis added.]

- *After filing the jurisdictional response, by virtue of the word "may" in Rule 21-8(1), the Australian Defendants were not obliged to proceed in accordance with Rule 21-8(1)(a)-(c). In my view, in choosing to file a substantive response to civil claim, in order to maintain the attornment immunity provided in Rule 21-8(5), they were required to comply with Rule 21-8(1)(c) by alleging that this Court lacks jurisdiction to hear these claims. Accordingly, I conclude that the Australian Defendants have attorned to the jurisdiction of this Court. Having done so, they cannot now attempt to "unattorn" themselves, and an extension of time as requested by them does not assist their position on the issue of*

[Emphasis added.]

- *I adopt that analysis in this*

- *Schiele's lack of response to the July 2018 Notice to Admit triggers Rule 7-7(2) of the Supreme Court Civil Rules, B.C. Reg. 168/2009.*

- *I find that pursuant to Rule 7-7(2) Mr. Schiele is deemed to have admitted:*

1. *he is the owner of the brainsyntax.com website;*

1. *he operates this website;*

- *Holden wrote to him on January 10, 2017, asking that the posts written by Mr. Hanlon be removed from his website;*

1. *he did not remove these posts after being made aware that Ms. Holden wanted them removed from com.*

- *Further, Mr. Schiele is deemed to have admitted that the following articles were posted oncom:*

1. *article entitled "Diana Holden has been targeting me since late 2011 when I was a Law Student" at(d);*

1. *article entitled "Freedom of Speech Under Attack" at (j);*

- *article entitled "Intimidation Tactics of Diana Holden" at (l); and*

1. *article entitled "Criminal Harassment (AKA Stalking) Laws in Canada" at (m).*

- *With respect to the accessibility to the brainsyntax.com website, Laurie McGrath, who works as a skip-tracer in Ontario, testified that, in the fall of 2017, she went onto the brainsyntax.com website to see if she could find the articles that*

Mr. Hanlon had posted. Although the posts had been the subject of the interim injunction and had been removed from the website by then, she simply registered with her email address and was granted access to the website. I accept her testimony on this point.

- Although Mr. Schiele is deemed to have admitted that the four articles were posted on brainsyntax.com, importantly, Mr. Schiele did not admit that the articles were published de novo. The only article that was originally posted on brainsyntax.com is the article entitled "Dianna Holden has been targeting me since late 2011 when I was a Law Student", described at para. 87 of these

- There is no evidence before the Court regarding the publication of the other three articles on brainsyntax.com. In admitting that the other three articles were posted on brainsyntax.com, Mr. Schiele has not admitted the form of the posting or that the text of articles were reproduced and published in their entirety as opposed to in the form of a hyperlink to the original articles on other websites. There is no evidence before the Court of the content or form of the posted materials on brainsyntax.com.

- On the second component of the legal test for publication, I recognize that there is no properly admissible evidence as to whether anyone read the article entitled "Dianna Holden has been targeting me since late 2011 when I was a Law Student", nor any evidence of the number of views that it has generated on

brainsyntax.com. However, to find that there has been no publication of the article in British Columbia would be to ignore the realities of 21st century communication and internet-based publications: Chow at para. 85, citing Bernstein at para. 94. While the evidence is thin on the extent of the publication of this article, I am satisfied that I can reasonably infer that this article was viewed on brainsyntax.com by at least one individual in British Columbia.

- Accordingly, I find that the plaintiffs have proven that Mr. Schiele published the one article entitled "Dianna Holden has been targeting me since late 2011 when I was a Law Student". They have not proven that Mr. Schiele published any other impugned

- The impugned statements that I have found to be defamatory that were published by Mr. Schiele are:

1. Holden is purporting to be a lawyer / harassed Mr. Hanlon with a false Facebook account / Law Society forced her to delete the account // has been harassing Mr. Hanlon since December 2011

1. Holden uttered veiled death threat to Mr. Hanlon

- Schiele is deemed to have admitted that the statements in the enumerated articles were false when they were published, are presently false and

that he knew they were false when he published them. In any case, with respect to these statements I have concluded that the defence of justification cannot prevail on the evidence before the Court. Additionally, I have ruled that the Charter argument does not afford the defendants any defence to this defamation action.

- In light of the admitted facts and not having established any defence, Mr. Schiele is liable for the defamatory statements he

DAMAGES

Legal Framework

- *Damages are awarded to compensate the plaintiff for the harm to his or her reputation caused by publication of the defamatory statement. The objective of a damage award for defamation is vindication of a plaintiff's reputation and to compensate a plaintiff for the unjustified injury to his or her self-worth and dignity: Weaver at para.*

- *General damages are presumed from the publication of a defamatory statement and need not be established by proof of actual loss and are assessed at large in light of the circumstances of the case: Hill v. Church of Scientology of Toronto, [1995] 2 S.C.R. 1130 at para. 164 [Hill]. Aggravated damages may be awarded where the plaintiff proves malice on the part of the defendant, and punitive damages where the degree of misconduct is so substantial that it offends the court's sense of*

- *I set out below the legal principles applicable to each category of damages as I summarized them in Lougheed Estate.*

General Damages

- In a defamation case, "the damages which are available to [a plaintiff] are damages at large not requiring [a plaintiff] to prove actual loss or injury": John v. Kim, 2007 BCSC 1224 at para.

- The phrase "at large" was defined in Drouillard v. Cogeco Cable Inc., 2007 ONCA 322 at para. 42, as follows (citing Broome v. Cassell & Co. Ltd., [1972] A.C. 1027 at 1073 (H.L.)):

The expression "at large" should be used in general to cover all cases where awards of damages may include elements for loss of reputation, injured feelings, bad or good conduct by either party, or punishment, and where in consequence no precise limit can be set in extent.

- As explained in Hill at para. 187, the assessment of damages flows from the particular confluence of the following elements in a given case: the nature and circumstances of the publication of the libel, the nature and position of the victim of the libel, the possible effects of the libel statement upon the life of the plaintiff, and the actions and motivations of the

- A similar list of relevant factors was identified in Leenen v. Canadian Broadcasting Corp. (2000), 48 O.R. (3d) 656 (Ont. S.C.J.) at para. 205, aff'd (2001), 54 O.R. (3d) 612 (Ont. C.A.), leave to appeal ref'd, [2001] S.C.C.A. No. 432:

1. the seriousness of the defamatory statement;

1. the identity of the accuser;

1. the breadth of the distribution of the publication of the libel;

1. republication of the libel;

1. the failure to give the audience both sides of the picture and not presenting a balanced view;

1. the desire to increase one's professional reputation or to increase ratings of a particular program;

1. the conduct of the defendant and defendant's counsel through to the end of trial;

1. the absence or refusal of any retraction or apology; and

1. the failure to establish a plea of

- The nature and character of the defamatory statement, the circumstances under which it was made and the extent to which it was disseminated may either enhance or reduce the damages awarded. A court may take into account the tone, language, content and gravity of the false statement, and the extent to which the defendant has sensationalized the statement: *Reichmann v. Berlin*, [2002] J. No. 2732 (Ont. S.C.J.) at para. 8 [*Reichmann*]. Ordinarily, the more widespread the publication, the larger the award of damages: *Reichmann* at para. 9.

- In the internet context, the mode and extent of publication must be considered with particular care: *Barrick Gold Corp. v. Lopehandia* (2004), 71 O.R. (3d) 416 (C.A.) at para. 31, 239 D.L.R. (4th) 577 [*Barrick Gold Corp.*]. The Court described the internet as "instantaneous, seamless, interactive, blunt, borderless and far reaching" (at para. 31), and said that "its interactive nature, its potential for being taken at face value, and its absolute and immediate worldwide ubiquity and accessibility" gave it greater potential than other media of communication to damage people's reputations (at para. 34).

- Nevertheless, where there is limited access to the website that published the defamatory statement and no evidence to show that the publications were being replicated throughout the internet, there is less likelihood that the damages will be as serious: Wilson v. Switlo, 2011 BCSC 1287 at paras. 502–503, aff'd 2013 BCCA 471 [Wilson]:

[502] The plaintiffs in addressing the issue of damages make specific mention of publication through the Internet. In my view, the Internet is simply another medium for publication, albeit one with the potential to be far more ubiquitous and accessible than other forms. Although it has the potential to increase damage awards significantly, this is not the inevitable effect of such publication.

[503] In the case at bar, the publications though made available on the Internet were "broadcast" to a limited audience. The "absolute and immediate worldwide ubiquity and accessibility" noted in Barrick was not necessarily present to the same degree here. Presumably, potential readers of the publications would have had to access the [British Columbia Utilities Commission] site to read the material in the first place. This is a far cry from publication of defamatory material on a frequently assessed internet message board, as in Barrick. There was no evidence that the publications were being replicated throughout theInternet.

- The reputation, prominence and professional standing of the plaintiff are important factors in the assessment of damages. Thus, in Hill for example, the Court found the vital importance of reputation to a lawyer to be a significant factor in its assessment. Certain individuals may hold elevated reputational status due to their public roles or notoriety. Numerous authorities have recognized the particular vulnerability of persons holding elected office to charges against their reputation and character given that their positions depend on the confidence of those who voted for them: see, for example, Lawson v. Burns, [1975] 1 W.W.R. 171 (B.C.S.C.) at

para. 53, and Snyder v. Montreal Gazette Ltd. (1978), 87 D.L.R. (3d) 5 (Que. C.S.) at para. 41.

- It has been recognized that damage caused by defamatory statements within a particular community may have a much more pervasive and far-reaching impact than statements made at large: Chow at para.

Aggravated Damages

- Aggravated damages may be awarded in circumstances where the defendant's conduct has been particularly high-handed or oppressive, thereby increasing the plaintiff's humiliation and anxiety arising from the defamatory statement:

Hill at para. 188. In order to award aggravated damages, the court must find that the defendant was motivated by actual malice, which increased the injury to the plaintiff, either by spreading further afield the damage to the reputation of the plaintiff or by increasing the mental distress and humiliation of the plaintiff: Hill at para.

- The Court explained that malice may be established by intrinsic evidence derived from the defamatory statement itself and the circumstances of its publication, or by extrinsic evidence pertaining to the surrounding circumstances, which demonstrate that the defendant was motivated by an unjustifiable intention to injure the plaintiff. In Hill, the Court continued at para. 191:

There are a number of factors that a jury may properly take into account in assessing aggravated damages. For example, was there a withdrawal of the libellous statement made by the defendants and an apology tendered? If there was, this may go far to establishing that there was no malicious conduct on the part of the defendant warranting an award of aggravated damages.

The jury may also consider whether there was a repetition of the libel, conduct that was calculated to deter the plaintiff from proceeding with the libel action, a prolonged and hostile cross-examination of the plaintiff or a plea of justification which the defendant knew was bound to fail. The general manner in which the defendant presented its case is also relevant. Further, it is appropriate for a jury to consider the conduct of the defendant at the time of the publication of the libel. For example, was it clearly aimed at obtaining the widest possible publicity in circumstances that were the most adverse possible to the plaintiff?

[Emphasis added.]

- The burden of proving malice is on the plaintiff. Malice, which focuses on the personal motives of the defendant, is not confined to its common meaning of personal spite or ill will, although these are its most obvious manifestations. Malice includes any indirect motive or ulterior purpose other than the public interest that would otherwise give rise to the applicable defence: Cherneskey v. Armadale Publishers Ltd., [1979] 1 S.C.R. 1067 at

- Madam Justice Kirkpatrick reviewed several leading authorities on malice in Smith v. Cross, 2009 BCCA 529, before quoting from a text that conveniently distilled the circumstances in which a finding of malice can be made:

[34] In Canadian Libel and Slander Actions (Toronto: Irwin Law, 2004) at 299,
R.D. McConchie and D.A. Potts reduce this statement to a helpful framework for the categories under which a finding of malice can be made. A defendant is actuated by malice if he or she publishes the comment:

1. Knowing it was false; or

2. With reckless indifference whether it is true or false; or

- For the dominant purpose of injuring the plaintiff because of spite or animosity; or

1. For some other dominant purpose which is improper or indirect, or also, if the occasion is privileged, for a dominant purpose not related to the

More than one finding can be present in a given case (McConchie and Potts at 299).

- The British Columbia Court of Appeal in *Kazakoff v. Taft*, 2018 BCCA 241 [*Kazakoff*], observed that, in the trial decision, some of the grounds for the award of aggravated damages overlapped with the grounds for the general damages

The Court cautioned trial judges regarding awarding double compensation at para. 50:

[50] I observe that the first two of the three reasons given for the award of aggravated damages duplicate reasons given to support the award of general damages. In my view, it would be preferable to consider these factors only once in making an award of compensatory damages to avoid the risk of double compensation.

See also *Brown v. Cole* (1998), [1999] 61 B.C.L.R. (3d) 1 (C.A.) at para. 100, *Nazerali v. Mitchell*, 2018 BCCA 104 at paras. 74-76 [*Nazerali*]; *Kazakoff* at paras. 51-54.

- *Aggravated damages awards will presumptively be less than the amount of general damages, except in extraordinary circumstances: Nazerali at para.*

Punitive Damages

- *Punitive damages may be awarded when the defendant's misconduct is so malicious and high-handed that it offends the court's sense of decency. Punitive damages, unlike general and aggravated damages, are not compensatory in nature, but rather are in the nature of a fine, which is meant to deter the defendant and others from engaging in similar conduct: Hill at para. 196. Punitive damages are to be awarded when the sum of general and aggravated damages is insufficient to achieve these objectives: Nazerali at para. 91.*

Assessed Jointly or Individually

- *It is a well-established principle that all persons who are involved in the commission of a joint tort are jointly and severally liable for the damages caused by the tort: Hill at para.*

- The leading authority on joint liability, or concerted action liability, is the decision of the Supreme Court of Canada in Botiuk v. Toronto Free Press Publications Ltd., [1995] 3 S.C.R. 3. The Court explained the concept of joint tortfeasors in these terms:

> [74] In [John G. Fleming,] The Law of Torts, 8th ed. [(Sydney: Law Book, 1992)], Fleming discusses the concept of joint concurrent tortfeasors. He states this at p. 255:
> A tort is imputed to several persons as joint tortfeasors in three instances: agency, vicarious liability, and concerted action. The first two will be considered later. The critical element of the third is that
>
>> those participating in the commission of the tort must have acted in furtherance of a common design.......................... Broadly speaking, this
>
> means a
>
>> conspiracy with all participants acting in furtherance of the wrong, though it is probably not necessary that they should realise they are committing a tort.
>
> [Cory J.'s emphasis.]

- Recently, the Ontario Court of Appeal, in Rutman v. Rabinowitz, 2018 ONCA 80, underscored that the determination of concerted action liability turns on the particular facts of any given case:

> [34] The difficulty, of course, is determining the degree of involvement or connection necessary to meet the requirements of concerted action liability. Canadian authorities suggest that

concerted action liability arises when a tort is committed in furtherance of a common design or plan, by one party on behalf of or in concert with another party: see Lewis N. Klar & Cameron S.G. Jefferies, Tort Law, 6th ed. (Toronto: Thomson Reuters, 2017), at p. 657;

 G.H.L. Fridman, The Law of Torts in Canada, 3rd ed. (Toronto: Carswell, 2010), at p. 856. In The Law of Torts, 10th ed. (Sydney: Thomson Reuters, 2011), at p. 302, Fleming puts it this way: "[k]nowingly assisting, encouraging or merely being present as a conspirator at the commission of the wrong would suffice, so too would any form of 'inducement, incitement orpersuasion' which procures the commission of the wrong." And, W. Page Keeton, in Prosser and Keeton on the Law of Torts, 5th ed. (Minnesota: West Publishing Co., 1984), at p. 323, states:

 All those who, in pursuance of a common plan or design to commit a tortious act, actively take part in it, or further it by cooperation or request, or who lend aid or encouragement to the wrongdoer, or ratify and adopt the wrongdoer's acts done for their benefit, are equally liable.

 [35] The key point is that concerted action liability is a fact-sensitive concept. Lord Neuberger emphasized as much in Sea Shepherd, at para. 56, reiterating Bankes LJ's admonition from "Koursk" (The), Re, [1924] P.

 140 (Eng. C.A.), at p. 151 that "[i]t would be unwise to attempt to define the necessary amount of connection", and that each case "must depend on its own circumstances". We agree.

[Emphasis added.]

- With these general principles on damages in mind, I turn to consider the circumstances of this

Position of the Parties

Ms. Holden

- Holden seeks general damages of $75,000, aggravated damages of

$15,000, and punitive damages of $25,000.

- On the question of the entitlement of the corporate plaintiffs to a damages award, the plaintiffs, in their submissions, expressed their position as follows:

The damages should, be in large part, to Ms. Holden personally. She operates her companies as a licensed private investigator. She has a licence, as does her company and most of the libel is against her. However, some of the libel is against the two corporate plaintiffs. There should be a damage award as sought in the Plaintiffs' closing argument in favour of the Plaintiff and separate smaller sums of damages in favour of the two corporate Plaintiffs since they were likewise damaged by Mr. Hanlon *independent of his attacks on Ms. Holden. Mr. Hanlon's attacks were so damaging that Ms.*

Holden had to change her company and personal names.

An appropriate sum of damages in favour of the corporate Plaintiffs would be half the sum awarded to Ms. Holden.

In the alternative, all the damages should be awarded to Ms. Holden personally.

- Holden also submits that Mr. Schiele ought to be jointly and severally liable for the damages, as he has published "essentially every article".

Mr. Hanlon

- Since Mr. Hanlon's primary contention is that the impugned statements were true, his submissions on damages were limited. Mr. Hanlon underscored that

Ms. Holden provided no evidentiary basis to support the claim for damages for loss of business revenue. He points out Ms. Holden had only commenced operating her private investigation business in July 2016, and it is unlikely that any conduct on his behalf could have negatively affected the company's business. Moreover, he maintains that the actual cause of any business losses was Ms. Holden's poor business practices and difficulties with retention of employees.

- Hanlon also contends that, despite significant memberships in the various social media communities in which he posted, there is no evidence of the number of

individuals who read his postings nor any evidence of any negative reaction to those postings.

Assessment of Damages Against Mr. Hanlon

- I have concluded earlier in these Reasons that Ms. Holden is the only plaintiff who has established a claim in defamation. Accordingly, the assessment of damages against Mr. Hanlon that follows pertains only to Ms.

- In assessing the quantum of compensatory damages, I have considered the following factors:

- The allegations in the impugned statements are serious allegations against Ms. Holden. Integrity and ethical standards are crucial to the reputation of a private investigator and the skip tracing businesses in which she was engaged. In particular, Mr. Hanlon made unfounded allegations of serious criminal

- Hanlon made these statements about Ms. Holden as another security professional engaged in the private investigation business.

- The evidence establishes the publication of the impugned statements had an adverse impact on Ms. Holden personally. She suffered humiliation, anxiety, and loss of sleep as a result of the false publications. The fact that she changed her name, changed her company's name and reorganized the operating structure of her businesses fortifies my conclusion in this

- With respect to the breadth of the distribution of the publication of the libel, the evidence establishes that Mr. Hanlon published the impugned statements in various social media platforms that had the potential to be widely viewed. Further, the posts were visible for approximately one year, up until the interim injunction was granted, as which point it appears that the posts were removed. However, as observed by Mr. Justice Punnett in Wilson at

para. 502, publication on the Internet does not inevitably result in a significant damage award.

- *Overall, the evidence adduced on the extent of the readership of the impugned statements was thin. The evidence establishes that there were negative comments by various individuals on the "Intimidation Tactics of Dianna Holden" link that Mr. Hanlon posted to the Canada Court Watch Facebook group at (l). The various posts may well have been viewed by individuals conducting internet searches of prospective private investigators in the Lower Mainland. It can reasonably be inferred that these searches would have found Mr. Hanlon's impugned publications. While the precise extent of the readership cannot be ascertained, balancing the evidence as a whole, I find it more likely than not that the extent of the readership was*

- *The features of the internet described by the Ontario Court of Appeal in Barrick Gold Corp. at paras. 30-31, 33-34 - its "interactive nature, its potential for being taken at face value, and its absolute worldwide ubiquity and accessibility" - were not present to the degree established in the cases where a large damages award was made. The only republication of*

Hanlon's publications on the Internet, albeit considerable, was by largely Mr. Hanlon himself.

- *Pursuant to the interim injunction issued in October 2017, the impugned statements were removed from all the pertinent internet sites on which they had been published. Thereafter, the impugned statements were no longer available to be*

- In her submissions, Ms. Holden emphasized the negative effects on her businesses that was occasioned by Mr. Hanlon's tortious conduct. According to Ms. Holden, in the two weeks after she obtained her private investigator's licence,

she made approximately $13,000. She maintains that after the impugned statements were published, she encountered difficulties attracting clients. Potential clients questioned her about the publications on the Internet. She experienced difficulties retaining employees. According to Ms. Holden this also impacted her skip tracing business but to a lesser extent. In an apparent attempt to mitigate her losses,

Ms. Holden hired a marketing assistant and combined her private investigation

business with her skip-tracing business. Ms. Holden candidly acknowledged that, for the most part, her private investigation business had recovered by the time this matter had proceeded to trial in 2018.

- In the absence of sufficiently reliable evidence I am not persuaded that

Ms. Holden has established that there was a high demand for private investigators in the Abbotsford area at the material time. Furthermore, Ms. Holden produced no financial records or other documentary evidence that would support her claim for the loss of revenue or that would otherwise support her claim for business loss. In cases such as Chow where a substantial damage award was made, there were financial records produced by the corporate plaintiff to substantiate the claim that the plaintiff suffered business losses. Mr. Justice Weatherill found that the publications had a "devastating effect on the plaintiff's business" (at para. 119).

- Holden's private investigation business was a fledging business when Mr. Hanlon embarked on his online campaign to discredit her. Nonetheless, and balancing the evidence as a whole, I accept that in addition to emotional distress and humiliation Ms. Holden suffered some loss of business income as a result of the publication of the impugned statements. I accept that there was damage to her reputation and some economic damage that cannot be expressly proven, which are appropriately compensated in a claim for general damages.

- It bears emphasis that general damages are "at large" in defamation cases. While the authorities are instructive, defamation cases turn on their own unique facts and there is little to be gained from a detailed comparison of libel cases: Hill at

para. 187.

- On a balanced consideration of the factors that inform the assessment, I award Ms. Holden compensatory damages of $20,000 against Mr.

- *This award of damages is intended to compensate Ms. Holden for her personal distress and tarnished reputation as well as for any possible economic or business loss, which may have resulted but cannot be expressly*

Aggravated Damages

- *Balancing the evidence as a whole and applying the applicable legal framework, I find that Mr. Hanlon was actuated by*

- *It bears emphasis a plaintiff can succeed in establishing malice if she or he demonstrates on a balance of probabilities that a defendant recklessly published statements that were*

- *Hanlon published the impugned statements with a reckless indifference as to whether they were true or false. He was not merely careless with regard to the truth. Moreover, he insisted on pursuing the justification defence through to trial without a reasonable evidentiary basis for doing so. He published the statements on numerous occasions on numerous* social media platforms. The preponderance of the evidence supports a finding that Mr. Hanlon's primary motivation was to destroy Ms. Holden's reputation. In order to do so, he engaged in an internet vendetta over many months. On his own admission, his goal was to publish the posts broadly to the public in the Lower Mainland so as to deter members of the public from hiring Ms. Holden. He never corrected any of the statements nor made any apology. The repetitious nature of Mr. Hanlon's allegations and the mode and extent of the publication aggravated the public embarrassment and harm caused to Ms. Holden.

- Balancing all of the factors that inform the assessment, I make an award of

$7,500 for aggravated damages. Those individuals who maliciously damage reputations by engaging in the wrongful dissemination of actionable defamatory statements on the internet must provide financial redress for the adverse impact of their unlawful conduct. This recognizes that the unfairly created stigma associated with unsubstantiated allegations can never be wholly undone.

Punitive Damages

- It bears emphasis that punitive awards are awarded where the defendant's conduct is so malicious and highhanded that it offends the court's sense of decency: Hill at para. 196.

- I am not persuaded that Mr. Hanlon's conduct was sufficiently egregious to warrant sanction through a punitive damages award. Furthermore, I am satisfied that the sum of the general and aggravated damages I have awarded is sufficient to deter Mr. Hanlon and others from engaging in similar tortious

- All things considered I conclude that the circumstances of this case do not merit an award of punitive

Assessment of Damages Against Mr. Schiele

- The Court did not have the benefit of any submissions from Mr. Schiele, as he did not appear at trial.

- *As a first step in the analysis, the evidence does not support a finding that Mr. Schiele ought to be jointly and severally liable for any damages assessed against Mr. Hanlon on the grounds that he published "essentially every article", as is asserted by the*

- *I have set out earlier in these Reasons the defamatory statements in the single article published on brainsyntax.com for which Mr. Schiele is liable. I must assess the quantum of damages that flow only from the defamatory statements published in that*

- *I find that for those statements he did publish, Mr. Schiele is jointly and severally liable for the damages caused by their publication. The evidence as a whole supports a finding that Mr. Hanlon and Mr. Schiele were joint tortfeasors acting in furtherance of a common*

- *Importantly, however, the number of defamatory statements published by Mr. Schiele is significantly less than those published by Mr.*

- As I stated earlier, Ms. Holden is not required to prove loss in order to recover general damages for defamation. Weighing the evidence in light of the applicable legal principles, I conclude that $1,000 of the damages awarded against Mr. Hanlon should be assessed jointly and severally against Mr. Hanlon and Mr.

- There is not a sufficient evidentiary basis to make an award of aggravated damages against Mr.

INJUNCTION

- In addition to damages, the plaintiffs seek a permanent injunction restraining Mr. Hanlon and Mr. Schiele from publishing the defamatory material or any material similar to it.

- In Pan v. Gao, 2018 BCSC 2137 at paras. 453–464, Madam Justice Sharma, after canvassing the authorities, concluded that granting an injunction on future publication is "an exceptional remedy which will only be imposed by the courts in the clearest of cases".
- All things considered, I conclude that the totality of the evidence supports a finding that, in the absence of an injunc-

tion, there is a substantial likelihood that both defendants would continue to publish the defamatory statements. I conclude that a permanent injunction in the following term should be issued:

> Lee Hanlon ("Hanlon"), any agent of Hanlon's, Vincent Schiele ("Schiele"), and any agent of Schiele, SHALL BE ENJOINED FROM either directly or indirectly, writing, publishing, posting or in any way distributing or making public any accusatory or disparaging allegations regarding the honesty, trustworthiness or alleged improper behaviour of Dianna Holden ("Holden"), NPL Services Inc. ("NPL") and National People Locator in any forum of any kind whatever and enjoining Hanlon and Schiele from directing or assisting others in writing, publishing, posting to the Internet or in any way distributing or making public such allegations and without limiting the generality of the foregoing, from posting allegations similar to those made in the following prior postings:
>
> 1. Posting dated July 8, 2016 on Craigslist entitled "SCAM ALERT: NPL SERVICES";
> 2. All posting made on the Facebook group "United Victims of Dianna Holden";
> 3. Posting in September 2016 on Facebook group titled "WTF Abbotsford" respecting Holden;
> 4. Posting made in October 2016 titled "Charter of Rights Freedom of Speech Under Attack", that was either edited or reposted on December 25, 2016;
> 5. Posting made on or around May 14, 2017 on the Facebook group "Veterans Transition Network";

6. Posting dated August 7, 2017 tiled "Beware of PI Con-Artists";

1. Posting dated August 21, 2017 titled "Freedom of Speech Under Attack";
2. Posting dated August 26, 2017 on the Facebook group "Canada Court Watch";
3. Posting dated September 4, 2017 titled "Intimidation Tactics by Dianna Holden";
4. Posting dated September 10, 2017 titled "Criminal Harassment (AKA Stalking) Laws in Canada"; and
5. Various posts on Facebook, Brainsyntax and elsewhere respecting Holden and

- The parties have leave to apply to vary the terms of the injunction as circumstances may

COSTS

- In all the circumstances, it is appropriate to permit the parties to argue the issue of costs after the release of these Reasons for Judgment. It may be that one or more of the parties will have submissions to make concerning costs that relate to

pre-trial offers to settle.

- Because I retired as a judge of this Court effective January 1, 2019, if the parties wish to make submissions concerning costs, they should contact Supreme Court Scheduling to arrange a hearing date before another judge of this

"Dardi J."

~ Twelve ~

EPILAGUE

When you decide to write a book, pertaining to a matter so personal such as being defamed, it is a difficult choice. You find yourself wondering, should I include, this should I include that. You also are left wondering whether you should change all the names of the parties involved.

I decided to not change the names of the parties involved, as I believe in transparency. All of the statements made in this book are completely factual. Information contained in this book such as the trial judgement is published in the public domain as it is a cited court decision, which is available to the public. Therefore, I chose to not change the contents of the court decision in any capacity.

Throughout the ordeal with Lee Hanlon, one thing that truly became apparent. You cannot control what others say or do. You further cannot control what ones opinion of you is. All you can do is be the best person you can be and treat others as you would want to be also treated.

Even when someone wrongs you, reciprocating that wrong, does not bring justice, it just brings further pain. You need to stand up for yourself in a positive manner, and regardless of who wrongs you just make sure you don't stoop to their level, because in the end you will win.

I won against Lee Hanlon, I did not stoop to his level, I did not become the person he chose to describe on paper. I am a very respectful human being, that just happens to use her investigative skills to help others.

I believe there is a purpose for everything on Earth, there is a reason for everything that happens. Although you may not like what happens or what is happening, I truly believe there is a reason. I take away from every situation I encounter, as an educational tool.

This is how I get through my day. How do you get through yours?

The End

www.ingramcontent.com/pod-product-compliance
Lightning Source LLC
Chambersburg PA
CBHW071907290426
44110CB00013B/1316